For Nancy

Charity, justice, and evangelization are thus the normal consequences of liturgical celebration.

—*Sing to the Lord: Music in Divine Worship*, 9

Glorify the Lord by Your Life

Catholic Social Teaching and the Liturgy

Bernard Evans

LTP

LITURGY
TRAINING
PUBLICATIONS

Nihil Obstat
Rev. Mr. Daniel G. Welter, JD
Chancellor
Archdiocese of Chicago
March 5, 2020

Imprimatur
Most Rev. Ronald A. Hicks
Vicar General
Archdiocese of Chicago
March 5, 2020

This book was edited by Danielle A. Noe. Michael A. Dodd was the production editor, Anna Manhart was the designer, and Luis Leal was the production artist.

Art by Cody F. Miller.

24 23 22 21 20   1 2 3 4 5

Printed in the United States of America

Library of Congress Control Number: 2020931303

ISBN: 978-1-61671-569-4

GLYL

CONTENTS

INTRODUCTION   VII

THEME 1 The Life and Dignity of
the Human Person   1

THEME 2 The Call to Family, Community,
and Participation   11

THEME 3 Rights and Responsibilities   23

THEME 4 The Option for the Poor
and Vulnerable   33

THEME 5 The Dignity of Work
and the Rights of Workers   45

THEME 6 Solidarity   57

THEME 7 Care for God's Creation   67

CATHOLIC SOCIAL TEACHING DOCUMENTS   77

INTRODUCTION

For I was hungry and you gave me food, I was thirsty and you gave me drink, a stranger and you welcomed me, naked and you clothed me, ill and you cared for me, in prison and you visited me. . . . Whatever you did for one of these least brothers of mine, you did for me.

—Matthew 25:35–36, 40

What Is Catholic Social Teaching?

How should Christians respond to climate change? How should they determine what is a just wage today? Or, what to do about frequent mass shootings? These and many other issues are debated today with passion and conviction, but where do we turn for moral norms to guide us in these discussions?

Jesus told us to love our neighbor and he showed us what that love should look like. The Parable of the Good Samaritan tells us that we are to help a hurting stranger, even one we may despise (see Luke 10:29–37). The Parable of the Last Judgement says that loving our neighbor means we feed her when she is hungry, give drink when she is thirsty, care for her when she is sick, visit her when she is in prison, provide clothing when she is without, and welcome her when she stands before us as an immigrant or a refugee (see Matthew 25:31–46).

We face these same challenges today and it should not be that difficult to look to Jesus' many encounters with people in need in order to know how to respond. However, we also face issues that are not depicted in the Scriptures. The Gospels do not include a parable of the good environmentalist. Jesus did not debate with the Pharisees about gun control. Even questions surrounding poverty, hunger, and workers' wages are very different today than they were during Jesus' time.

Making direct—and sometimes simplistic—applications of Scripture quotes to answer complex twenty-first century issues carries obvious risks. The Gospel accounts, Acts of the Apostles, and the letters of St. Paul were written with an eye to forming and guiding the earliest Christian communities. These same texts continue to form us as Christians today. The Bible is absolutely necessary to form our understanding of Christianity and how to live as Christ's disciples in a broken world. However, these biblical texts were never intended to answer complicated social, economic, and political questions. If the Gospel accounts and other Scripture texts do not specify contemporary situations, where do we go for moral directions? How should a Christian respond to challenges and situations found on today's social media news feed? How do we make the connection between hyphenate: first-century Scripture writings and twenty-first-century challenges that come with living in any society?

> The Church's social teaching is a rich treasure of wisdom about building a just society and living lives of holiness amidst the challenges of modern society. It offers moral principles and coherent values that are badly needed in our time. In this time of widespread violence and diminished respect for human life and dignity in our country and around the world, the Gospel of life and the biblical call to justice need to be proclaimed and shared with new clarity, urgency, and energy.
>
> —United States Catholic Bishops, *Sharing Catholic Social Teaching: Challenges and Directions*

The Church's long theological tradition is the first place to look for guidance in making that connection. Within the tradition, the most helpful sources for engaging in moral reflection about difficult issues are the social teachings of the Catholic Church. These teachings guide us in situations that are not found in the Scriptures and may not have been given much attention in the Church's early theological offerings.

To put it another way, Catholic social teachings guide us in *applying the Gospel* to today's social, economic, and political challenges. Catholic social teaching helps us answer the question: "What does it mean to be a disciple of Jesus Christ facing these problems in this time and place?" Every generation of Christians faces new hurdles to living the Gospel in a way that is faithful to Jesus' teachings. The teachings evolve and change as humanity evolves and changes. Issues that were addressed by the Church in earlier centuries might require a fresh moral analysis. Such is the case regarding women in the workplace, the human rights of the LBGTQ community, nations' responsibilities to refugees, as well as various aspects of what we now refer to as the environmental crisis. Still, other issues are the result of contemporary developments and requires the Church's response, such as nuclear war. It is the task of Catholic social teaching to offer moral guidance on how we should act in the face of these new problems as well as older ones with new insights. These instructions guide us in responding to contemporary challenges in ways that are consistent with the love Jesus says we must have for one another.

The Church's teachings, however, do not provide specific instructions for how to solve economic, cultural, and political problems. This is not their purpose. The teachings do not, for example, determine a just wage for twenty-first-century American workers. Nor do these teachings tell us how to deal with climate change. Rather, these teachings provide moral *principles* and a moral *framework* for considering such matters. The teachings seek to ensure that public debates and policies, consider moral factors along with those of an economic, political, and social nature.

So where do we find these Catholic social teachings? Most of them come to us as written documents, typically papal encyclicals, such Pope John Paul II's *On Social Concerns* (1987). Some come to us from the Second Vatican Council, such as *The Pastoral Constitution on the Church in the Modern World* (1965). Others are joint statements from the Word Synod of Bishops, such as *Justice in the World*

(1971), as well as apostolic exhortations, such as *A Call to Action* (1971).[1] In addition to these universal documents, others come from more local bishops' conferences, such as *Economic Justice for All* (1986). All of them can be found on various websites, including the Vatican website. A useful hard copy collection is that published by Orbis Books, *Catholic Social Thought: Encyclicals and Documents from Pope Leo XIII to Pope Francis.*

Each of the Catholic social documents typically focuses on one or a few major problems facing the world. The documents address these topics using Scripture and the broader theological tradition of the Catholic Church. The first social encyclical was written by Pope Leo XIII in 1891. *On the Condition of Labor* addressed the struggles of workers during the later stages of the industrial revolution. It speaks of the responsibilities and rights of all workers, including their right to unionize and to strike.

> Beloved, let us love one another, because love is of God; everyone who loves is begotten by God and knows God. Whoever is without love does not know God, for God is love.
>
> —1 John 4:7–8

From 1891 to the present, popes have issued such documents in response to different issues or challenges facing the world. Pope John XXIII, for example, presented *Peace on Earth* in 1963 which included a section on the threat of nuclear war. Pope Paul VI in 1967 wrote *On the Development of Peoples*, calling attention to the needs of poorer nations and the corresponding duties of countries with great wealth. More recently, Pope Francis wrote *On Care for Our Common Home*, the first papal encyclical to focus on the environment. These teachings provide moral principles and practical guidance. Catholic social teaching helps twenty-first-century Catholics engage challenges in a way that is faithful to Jesus' command to love our neighbor.

---

1. Vatican documents are originally promulgated (or published) in Latin and may often be referred to by their Latin title; however, for this work the English titles are used.

Catholic Social Teaching and the Liturgy

We might not often think about Catholic social teaching having much to do with liturgy, but the points of contact are many and they are deep. As already noted, these teachings guide us in how we are to live our communal and social lives. The Church's liturgy forms and helps us appreciate what it means to live as a disciple of Jesus Christ. In a general sense, the liturgy spells out who we are and why we should act as directed by the Catholic social documents. Recall the words of the dismissal, "Go in peace, glorifying the Lord by your life."

As we worship God through liturgical acts, we become ever more aware of our relationship to God and the expectations and responsibilities that flow from this relationship. The liturgy always reminds us that we are made in God's image and that we humans enjoy a sacred dignity that must be reflected in how we conduct our lives in the privacy of our homes and in the public square. The liturgy constantly points out that we are also broken and sinful beings in need of God's redeeming grace. Through symbols and ritual, public acts of worship lead us to recognize our capacity for accomplishing great things, our need for personal conversion, and our responsibility to help make changes in our shared social life. These, likewise, are some of the most fundamental beliefs expressed in Catholic social teaching.

> The liturgy is "the source and summit of the Christian life."
>
> —*Dogmatic Constitution on the Church*, 11

Although there are many expressions of the Church's liturgy—the sacraments, the Liturgy of the Hours, blessings—the best example of how the liturgy and Catholic social teaching are related can be found in the Sunday Mass, the Eucharistic celebration. There we worship, not as unrelated individuals, but as a people—a community that recognizes its shared identity in the Body of Christ. The Mass places before the worshipping community the needs and challenges of our society and world. This public worship reminds us of a point presumed in Catholic social teaching: the needs for which we pray become the focus of our care and action after we leave the liturgy. It is never enough to offer "thoughts and prayers." We must, likewise, act to help bring about that for which we pray.

The liturgical readings, especially the First Readings and Responsorial Psalms from the Old Testament, emphasize that if we wish to be in right relationship with God we must care for the widows, orphans, and strangers of our time. The prophets call us to work on behalf of people experiencing any sort of injustice such as poverty and hunger as well as persons who are homeless or experiencing discrimination.

The proclamation from the New Testament (the Second Reading and the Gospel) illustrate Jesus' special love for the poor and remind us how, at the start of his public ministry, he proclaimed freedom for the oppressed. Most importantly, Jesus mandated that loving God means also loving our neighbor. This love must bring practical relief to anyone who suffers. The readings proclaimed at the liturgy and the preaching that expounds upon these readings call us to act in society in ways that are also called for in Catholic social teaching.

The Universal Prayer follows the readings and the homily. Petitions are offered for specific needs: the Church, the world, the oppressed, and the local community. These petitions call to mind the needs of our world and inspire the gathered faithful to go forth from the liturgy and help to change the lives of those who are suffering and share with them the love of God.

The Liturgy of the Eucharist is a sign of unity and a transformative encounter with Christ. Those who receive his broken body are changed to heal a broken world. But, it is also an act of thanksgiving to God for having restored our relationship with him, with our neighbor, and with all of creation. We go forth from Sunday Mass willing to help rid the human family of the strife, tensions, and injustices that divide us. We return to our communities seeking to change whatever contradicts what we have just celebrated in the Eucharist. Our Church's social teachings guide us in this task.

In his 2006 encyclical, *God Is Love*, Pope Benedict XVI reflected on this connection between the Mass and the kind of social engagement called for in the Church's social documents. "A Eucharist which does not pass over into the concrete practice of love is intrinsically fragmented" (14).[2] Caring for people with any need—widows and orphans, prisoners, and those who are sick—"is as essential to [the Church] as the ministry of the sacraments and preaching of the Gospel" (22).

Acts of charity and justice are intrinsic to who we are as Christians and what it means to be Church—a Eucharistic people. We must not take part in the Eucharist and then ignore the problems of our world, especially those which divide the human community.

Public worship moves us to do exactly what Catholic social teaching directs us to do—to challenge injustices in our communities, in our society, and in our world. The liturgy and Catholic social teaching prepare us to respond to any suffering or injury in the social, economic, and political sectors of our lives; reminding us of our deepest identity as sisters and brothers. All humans share a common dignity, were created to participate in community, and are empowered to do so to the fullest.

About This Book

This book is organized around the seven core themes of Catholic social teaching. In the mid-1990s, retired Archbishop John Roach (St. Paul-Minneapolis) assembled the Task Force on Catholic Social Teaching and Catholic Education. One of the goals of this Task Force, under the direction of the United States Conference of Catholic Bishops, was to identify ways the Church could make her social teachings better known among parishioners of all ages.

---

2. The paragraphs in Church documents are numbered sequentially. The references throughout this resource refer to the corresponding paragraph numbers in the quoted document.

To that end the Task Force identified seven basic themes that can be found in most of the social documents. These themes, and the reflection of the bishops following the work of this Task Force, can be found in the 1998 publication *Sharing Catholic Social Teaching: Challenges and Directions*. These seven key themes are at the very center of the Catholic social tradition, and they offer a starting point for engaging the Church's social teachings:

1. The Life and Dignity of the Human Person

2. The Call to Family, Community, and Participation

3. Rights and Responsibilities

4. The Option for the Poor and Vulnerable

5. The Dignity of Work and the Rights of Workers

6. Solidarity

7. Care for God's Creation

The following seven chapters focus on these themes, first explaining them and then reflecting briefly on how the Church's liturgy expresses each theme.[3] The content is grounded in Scripture, Catholic social teaching documents, and quotations from the saints. Each chapter begins with a quote from the Mass illustrating each theme and its connection to the liturgy. May these prayers help you reflect more deeply upon these important themes of Catholic social teaching and how these themes will impact your life of faith.

---

3. Most of the references and citations in these chapters are from Vatican documents, especially the social encyclicals. Others are drawn from more local Church documents, such as the United States Conference of Catholic Bishops' pastoral letter, *Economic Justice for All*. Although these latter sources are not "universal Church documents," they are valuable for their application of the principles of Catholic social teaching to the North American context. If you are interested in reading the documents referenced throughout this work, they are available online.

About the Author

Bernard Evans, PHD, is a retired faculty member at St. John's University, Collegeville, Minnesota, where he served as associate dean for faculty in the School of Theology. Evans also occupied the Virgil Michel Ecumenical Chair in Rural Social Ministries, teaching courses on Christian social ethics, environmental theology, and ministry in rural communities. His most recent publications include the books *Lazarus at the Table: Catholics and Social Justice* (2006); *Vote Catholic? Beyond the Political Din* (2008); *Stewardship: Living a Biblical Call* (2014); as well as a chapter, "Care for Creation," in *A Vision of Justice*, edited by Ron Pagnucco and Susan Crawford Sullivan (2014), all published by Liturgical Press. He also contributed to *The Liturgy and Catholic Social Teaching: Participation in Worship and the World* (2019) published by Liturgy Training Publications.

God created mankind in his image;
in the image of God he created them;
male and female he created them.

—Genesis 1:27

The Life and Dignity of the Human Person

God, who gave one origin to all peoples
and willed to gather from them one family for yourself,
fill all hearts, we pray, with the fire of your love
and kindle in them a desire
for the just advancement of their neighbor,
that, through the good things which you richly bestow
      upon all,
each human person may be brought to perfection,
every division may be removed,
and equity and justice may be established in human society.

—Collect, Mass for the Progress of Peoples[1]

"God saw that it was good." In the first chapter of the first book of the Bible, we hear the story about God creating the heavens and the earth. At the end of each day, God looked upon what he had created and saw that it was good. This included all the wild and tame animals, everything that crept upon the ground, all that lived in the sea, and the birds of the air. All of this God created, and all of this God saw was good.

When we read this account of creation we can hardly miss the point that all life on this planet is a blessing. All of creation is a gift and is good because it belongs to and comes from God. At the very least, humans should treat all living beings with love, care, and

---

1. Masses may be celebrated for various needs and occasions. *The Roman Missal*—the ritual book that the priest uses to celebrate the Mass—includes these prayers, which have been approved by the Church for these purposes. The Mass for the Progress of Peoples is just one example of the many options provided in the Missal. Prayers from these special Masses are used to begin other chapters in this book.

respect. Even as we rely on other living creatures for our survival, we appreciate the regard they are due as fellow travelers on the journey to God. But there is one creature that holds a special place among all that God has made. On the final day of creation, God formed humans and declared that they were good. In creating women and men in his own image and likeness, God charged humanity with the responsibility of caring for all that he had created. Human beings are to watch over creation as God would do.

Made in the Image of God

What does it mean to be made in God's image? Does God look like you? Are you a "spitting image" of God? Probably not. To be made in God's image means that we reflect the most important characteristic associated with God: that God is love. And, this love is the reason for our existence. God created us through love, and through love continues to keep us in existence.

> This is my commandment: love one another as I love you.
>
> —John 15:12

Made in God's image means we too are able to love—to enter into caring and nurturing relationships. Humans have the capacity to go out of themselves and seek the good of others. We are able to bring new life to others. Because we have received God's infinite love, we can share that love with all our sisters and brothers.

The Dignity of Every Person

God endows all human beings with dignity and this belief grounds the Church's teaching about people and our responsibilities in society. "At the center of the Church's teaching on peace and at the center of all Catholic social teaching are the transcendence of God and the dignity of the human person. The human person is the clearest reflection of God's presence in the world" (*The Challenge of Peace: God's Promise and Our Response*, 15). Human dignity is a gift from God who empowers us to love others as he loves. In doing so, we are a reflection—the image—of our loving God.

Catholic social teaching emphasizes that appreciating our own dignity as created by God will affect the way in which we live. If we see within ourselves the reflection of God's image we are more likely to show concern for and be loving toward others. "This sense of responsibility will not be achieved unless people are so circumstanced that they are aware of their dignity and are capable of responding to their calling in the service of God and of humanity" (*Pastoral Constitution on the Church in the Modern World*, 31). This is an essential aspect of the Christian life—to seek God and reach out in love and service to our neighbor. Awareness of our own dignity puts both goals within reach.

Acknowledging our own human dignity is a necessary first step to recognizing the inherent dignity within others. This applies both to people living close to us and to those in far off nations whose appearance, beliefs, and lifestyles may differ greatly from our own. "There will be no peace nor justice in the world until they return to a sense of their dignity as creatures and sons of God, who is the first and final cause of all created being" (*Christianity and Social Progress*, 215). Until we recognize that *all* people—not just Christians—are created by God and endowed with dignity, peace and justice will not prevail.

Recognizing the dignity that is proper to all human beings is only the first step. We must also strive to develop the gifts that God has given to each individual person and use them for the good of the global community. Every person has a vocation—a calling from God. Every person is granted a set of qualities and talents to guide us in living our particular vocation. It is our responsibility to bring these gifts to fruition and to use them:

> **The glory of God is the human person fully alive.**
>
> —St. Irenaeus

In God's plan, every [person] is born to seek self-fulfillment, for every human life is called to some task by God. At birth a human being possesses certain aptitudes and abilities in germinal form, and these qualities are to be cultivated so that they may bear fruit. By developing these traits through formal education of personal effort, the individual works his [or her] way toward the goal set for him [or her] by the Creator. (*On the Development of Peoples*, 15)

A failure to develop and put these gifts to use makes it difficult for our lives to reflect God's image and give witness to our universal call to love. It becomes difficult to recognize our own dignity and that of anyone else in the human family.

Responding to God's call—living out our vocation—is not likely to be a straight path. Any one of us knows from experience that some days are better than others; that we sometimes move forward and sometimes backwards. That is the nature of human life which is marked by sinful human tendencies. But, there is always hope. As Pope Francis has said, "Human beings, while capable of the worst, are also capable of rising above themselves, choosing again what is good, and making a new start, despite their mental and social conditioning" (*On Care for Our Common Home*, 205).

So we move through life with joy and confidence that we can become the persons God calls us to be, that we can use well the talents we have received, and that we truly can reflect God's image to anyone we meet. This vocation can be supported or hindered by the living conditions in which we find ourselves. Enduring extreme poverty, for example, or living under brutal political conditions can make it very difficult to realize our human dignity (see *Pastoral Constitution on the Church in the Modern World*, 31). Struggling to survive on a daily basis can prevent persons from taking full responsibility for their lives and from becoming what God created them to be.

> **When we deal with each other, we should do so with the sense of awe that arises in the presence of something holy and sacred. For that is what human beings are: we are created in the image of God.**
>
> —*Economic Justice for All*, 28

Sacredness of Human Life

All humans enjoy universal and inviolable rights and duties. Because of this, every person must have ready access to all that is necessary for living a genuinely human life. At the very least, this includes food, clothing, housing, education, and work (see chapter 3 and chapter 5). We bear God's image throughout our lives and in every situation. We must, therefore, have whatever is needed for a life that reflects this outgoing love for others, this willingness to imitate God by saying yes to loving and caring relationships with others. Each life reflects the love of our creator God. This is why every person is to be protected, nurtured, and cherished. and no human life is to be ended by another human being.

> A society will be judged on the basis of how it treats its weakest members.
>
> —Pope St. John Paul II

For this reason the Catholic Church opposes any act that intentionally and directly leads to the death of another human. This includes acts of abortion aimed at ending the life of an unborn child. It includes euthanasia even when such acts are carried out for the purpose of ending suffering. It includes the death penalty because there is always hope that God's grace may bring about a conversion of heart in the one incarcerated (and because state officials no longer need to kill the worst criminals in order to protect society). In recent decades, Catholic teaching even cautions against the quick acceptance of war as a just act because it is the cause of countless innocent children, women, and men dying. While the legitimate right to self-defense is recognized—for individuals and nations— the Church reminds us that any discussion of a just war must begin with a presumption against war (see *The Challenge of Peace: God's Promise and Our Response*, 70).

Purposely ending another person's life is the result of the failure to recognize God's image within another human being. It is a failure to recognize that every human life is sacred from conception until God calls that person home—even when a person acts contrary to the love of God.

No person is perfect. Many of us commit acts that do not reflect the dignity with which we were endowed by God. We don't always live up to God's image. However, our merciful creator never stops loving us, even when we are sinful and engage in horrible acts against our brothers and sisters. Neither should we.

Connections to the Liturgy

Although many Catholics are not necessarily familiar with the documents about Catholic social teaching, they will encounter and be formed by the teachings regularly through participation in the liturgy. Our liturgical celebrations present many of the basic themes found in Catholic social teaching. They do so through symbols, ritual acts, Scripture readings, and prayers. When we celebrate the liturgy, especially the Mass, we see and hear direct and indirect references to the sacredness of human life and the dignity of the human person.

We gather together. Liturgy cannot take place without people. We come together from all walks of life—rich and poor, black and white, woman and man, elderly person and child, and so on. We worship God and give him thanks and praise for all that he has created is good! We are the People of God, dignified by our very life in God, and, baptized, Christ dwells within us. Indeed, Christ "is present . . . when the Church prays and sings" (*Constitution on the Sacred Liturgy*, 7).

> The Eucharist is the Sacrament of Love. It signifies Love. It produces love. The Eucharist is the consummation of the whole spiritual life.
>
> —St. Thomas Aquinas

As the gathered Body of Christ, certain actions point to our inherent dignity. We welcome all who come to worship and invite everyone to participate fully, actively, and consciously and, in an act of hospitality, we ensure that the assembly is able to do so. We dignify our own worship and the worship of others by sharing in common gestures, postures, and prayers. We are sprinkled with blessed water to remind us of our redemption. We are invited to hear God's Word and share in the Eucharist. We are incensed. We extend the sign of Christ's peace and are blessed to go forth and share this love with the entire created world. All of these aspects of the liturgy symbolically express the core belief that all persons are created in the image and likeness of God and therefore are given a special dignity as his adopted sons and daughters.

The prayer texts themselves are catechetical and form the gathered assembly in the Church's social teachings. We see this particularly in the prayers found in the Liturgy of the Eucharist. After the gifts are brought forward and the altar is prepared, we join our prayers to that of the priest in the Eucharistic Prayer. This great prayer of thanksgiving includes what is called the epiclesis, or the sending down of the Holy Spirit, so that the gifts of bread and wine may be changed into the Body and Blood of Christ. These words should be familiar to you, as a variation of this text is included in every Eucharistic Prayer: "by the same Spirit graciously make holy / these gifts we have brought to you for consecration" (Eucharistic Prayer III[2]). These words come just before the institution narrative. What may not be as evident is that there is a second epiclesis in which the Holy Spirit is called upon to transform us! "Humbly we pray / that, partaking of the Body and Blood of Christ, / we may be gathered into one by the Holy Spirit" (Eucharistic Prayer II). Worthy and dignified are we that we should be blessed by the Holy Spirit to do God's work in the world.

Each Eucharistic Prayer begins with a preface highlighting a particular aspect of the life of Christ and his plan for salvation. The priest often is required to pray a particular preface that the Church has assigned to a certain day or season. One of the two options for the Preface for the Solemnity of the Ascension of the Lord points to human dignity. We hear, "For after his Resurrection / he plainly appeared to all his disciples / and was taken up to heaven in their sight, / that he might make us sharers in his divinity." How privileged is human life to be able to share in Christ's divinity! How sacred is this life and how dignified are those who can look forward to eternal life with Christ! How comforting to know that as

---

2. The ten Eucharistic Prayers are named by number and purpose: Eucharistic Prayers I–IV, Eucharistic Prayers I and II for Reconciliation, and Eucharistic Prayers I–IV for Masses for Various Needs and Occasions (such as a wedding or human needs).

we travel this life's journey we are accompanied by Christ and marked as sharers in his divinity.

That sacred, dignified status of humanity is recognized again in Eucharistic Prayer III. We hear the celebrant offer the beautiful prayer to God, who through his "Son our Lord Jesus Christ" and "by the power and working of the Holy Spirit" gives "life to all things and make[s] them holy" (Eucharistic Prayer III). All of creation is holy—and so are we! This same prayer also acknowledges that God constantly gathers a people to himself. We are not simply part of God's holy creation—we have a special place within creation and God gathers us to himself. Human beings are made in God's image and possess a sacred dignity and are in relationship with him.

The fourth Eucharistic Prayer directly speaks of humankind's special status within all creation: "You formed man in your own image / and entrusted the whole world to his care" (Eucharistic Prayer IV). This text underscores what is repeated with regularity in Catholic social teaching: being made in the image of a loving creator is directly connected to our responsibility to care for creation. We watch over the world just as God would do. The dignity that we enjoy comes with the fearsome expectation that our interaction with the rest of the world will be marked by valuing, respecting, and protecting all that lives.

Other liturgical celebrations note the sacredness of human life and the dignity of every person. Through baptism, for example, each of us participates in Christ's death and resurrection. Baptized Christians enjoy a special dignity because they have been redeemed by Christ. Christians know that through Christ's life, death, and resurrection their relationships with God, neighbor, and all of creation has been restored. And yet this dignity is ultimately linked to the final goal in the journey of faith: "Human dignity rests above all on the fact that humanity is called to communion with God" (*Pastoral Constitution on the Church in the Modern World*, 19).

We take on a new life and enter into the Body of Christ—the Church. The sacrament of baptism bestows a nobility on everyone called into the Christian community. All the baptized enjoy this special status, and there is equality among all. As St. Paul wrote, among the baptized "there is neither Jew nor Greek, there is neither slave nor free person, there is not male and female; for you are all one in Christ Jesus" (Galatians 3:28).

Recognizing this equality among all—that we "are all one in Christ Jesus"—compels us to seek the good of all in the Church and especially defend the lives and dignity of every member. However, this love should be extended beyond the walls of the Church. We extend love to *all* people, wherever they live, and whatever they hold as religious beliefs. We do this because we recognize and rejoice that every human being is made in the image of God and that every human life is sacred.

Reflect ❋ Discuss ❋ Act

1. Give a practical example of how awareness of your human dignity makes a difference in your life.

2. Besides abortion, where have you recently seen a violation of human dignity and respect for life? How might you act or respond to this?

3. Our lives can be a witness to what we believe and to what we celebrate in our liturgies. How might your daily life promote respect for human dignity and for the sacredness of human life?

4. How might your participation in the Eucharist lead you to a better understanding of what Catholic social teaching says about the sacredness of human life and the dignity of the human person?

As each one has received a gift, use it to serve one another as good stewards of God's varied grace.

—1 Peter 4:10

The Call to Family, Community, and Participation

> O God, who have called us to participate
> in this most sacred Supper,
> in which your Only Begotten Son,
> when about to hand himself over to death,
> entrusted to the Church a sacrifice new for all eternity,
> the banquet of his love,
> grant, we pray,
> that we may draw from so great a mystery,
> the fullness of charity and of life.
>
> —Collect, Evening Mass of the Lord's Supper[1]

Human beings are social creatures. That is a fundamental belief in Catholic social teaching and, like human dignity, it provides the basis for communal living. Humans need and depend on one another. We look to one another for guidance and support. We expect friends and family members to challenge and bring out the best in us. Yes, sometimes this guidance is overdone. We might wish Aunt Anne wasn't so willing to give her advice and that our nosy neighbor would "mind his own business." Yet despite the occasional overbearing person in our life, we do understand that we need others and depend on these social relationships. Very few of us would do well living completely apart from others in isolation.

The Church also recognizes that we need others to complete our journey to God. In her *Pastoral Constitution on the Church in the*

---

1. This prayer is used at the Evening Mass of the Lord's Supper, a liturgy that celebrates the institution of the Eucharist and Jesus' command to do to others what he has done for us (see John 13:15).

Modern World, the Second Vatican Council acknowledged this in a beautiful statement about our salvation:

> God did not create people to live as individuals but to come together in the formation of social unity, so he "willed to make women and men holy and to save them, not as individuals without any bond between them, but rather to make them into a people who might acknowledge him and serve him in holiness." (32)

We are one people. We go to God together and along the way we look out for one another. As we move on this journey of faith, we find ourselves in various communities. We begin in families and attend schools. We join others in different workplace settings. We are citizens of villages, cities, and nations. Our life within these communities greatly influences our ability to grow as healthy human beings and as morally responsible persons. Life in community can help us become the persons God intends us to be.

There are two important aspects to participating in our communities and global society. The first is that we must promote the common good. The Second Vatican Council defined the *common good* as "the sum total of social conditions which allow people, either as groups or as individuals, to reach their fulfillment more fully and more easily" (*Pastoral Constitution on the Church in the Modern World*, 26). In other words, the common good is that collection of things that each of us needs for a dignified life: food, water, shelter, education, freedom of speech, and the practice of religion. The second is that every person contributes to the common good by using whatever gifts God has given to him or her. Citizens have a right to contribute to the true progress of their communities and to the common good according to their personal abilities (see *Pastoral Constitution on the Church in the Modern World*, 65). It is also their duty, or responsibility. This might be helping a neighbor think more positively about an ethnic minority group moving into the community. It could be as simple as giving to the local food pantry or volunteering to serve meals in a church program. It might be making

> We must love our neighbor as being made in the image of God and as an object of his love.
>
> —St. Vincent de Paul

a special effort during election campaigns to educate oneself about the candidates and then voting for those who recognize that the primary purpose of government is to promote the common good. This is living out our call to community.

During his earthly ministry, Jesus gave a clear command for his disciples to love God and love their neighbor: "'You shall love the Lord your God with all your heart, and with all your soul, with all your mind, and with all your strength. . . . You shall love your neighbor as yourself.' There is no greater commandment greater than these" (Mark 12:30–31). Love for God is expressed by how we love our neighbor rightly. Dorothy Day, an advocate of the poor and cofounder of the Catholic Worker Movement, once said that we "really only love God as much as [we] love the person [we] love the least." Catholic social teaching emphasizes that participating in our communities and seeking the common good is a *requirement* of justice and charity (love). No one is exempt from contributing. And no one should be satisfied with a "merely individualistic morality," as if our only moral obligation is to oneself and not to our sisters and brothers. Indeed, "all must consider it their sacred duty to count social obligations among their chief duties today and observe them as such" (*Pastoral Constitution on the Church in the Modern World*, 30).

Our redemption is not just something wonderful happening to individuals. Rather, redemption has a social dimension because Christ also redeems the social relations existing between individual persons. The acceptance of the Gospel requires and "invites us to receive God's love and to love him in return with the very love which is his gift, [and] brings forth in our lives and actions a primary and fundamental response: to desire, seek and protect the good of others" (*The Joy of the Gospel*, 178). For this very reason, we should have every confidence that we can help improve life in our own communities and anywhere people lack basic necessities. Through the redeeming actions of Christ, the ground has already been prepared for our contributions.

The United States Catholic Bishops reminded us that although the obligation to love our neighbor involves person-to-person contact, the obligation requires a broader "*social commitment* to the common good" (*Economic Justice for All*, "Introduction," 14, emphasis added). We love our neighbor by saying "Good morning" and by providing assistance when he or she lacks food or housing. We also love our neighbor by working to bring about higher wages so that she—and millions of workers like her—can afford to buy the food and shelter she needs on a daily basis. The call to community warns us that the Christian never seeks simply his or her own good or pursues a strictly individual morality. There is nothing wrong with following our interests and making sure we have what we and our dependents need for a modestly comfortable life. But it should not stop there. We answer this call when we respond as well to the needs of our neighbor and when we lend our talents and resources to building healthy communities. To this end, Pope John XXIII wrote that we should live in a common good morality and bring our "own interests with the needs of others" (*Peace on Earth*, 53).

Responsibility toward the common good does not just fall on the shoulders of individual Christians. Catholic social teaching repeatedly points out that the purpose of the state—the purpose of government at all levels—is to promote the welfare of society. The government must watch over the community and its various parts, defend human rights, maintain just social and economic structures, and initiate policies and structural changes as the needs arise (see *On Reconstructing the Social Order*, 25). Pope Paul VI could not have stated it more clearly: "Political power, which is the natural and necessary link for ensuring the cohesion of the social body, must have as its aim the achievement of the common good" (*A Call to Action*, 46).

> "You shall love the Lord your God with all your heart, with all your soul, with all your mind, and with all your strength. . . . You shall love your neighbor as yourself." There is no other commandment greater than these.
>
> —Mark 12:30-31

Every Christian must be ready to make those contributions as actions flowing from our faith. In the *Joy of the Gospel*, Pope Francis makes this point: "An authentic faith—which is never comfortable or completely personal—always involves a deep desire to change this world, to transmit values, to leave this earth somehow better than we found it" (183).

This task of building a better world is not only the duty of the individual Christian called to community. It is likewise a challenge facing the entire Church. As Pope Francis stated, "the Church 'cannot and must not remain on the sidelines in the fight for justice.' All Christians, their pastors included, are called to show concern for the building of a better world" (*The Joy of the Gospel*, 183).

Concern for the common good is not limited to individual communities—villages, nations, or communities of any other size. "Every group must take into account the needs and legitimate aspirations of every other group, and even those of the human family as a whole" (*Pastoral Constitution on the Church in the Modern World*, 26). Pope John Paul II developed this point in his encyclical *On Social Concerns*. He reflected upon how the more affluent and powerful nations must conduct themselves on the global scene: "A leadership role among nations," he wrote, "can only be justified by the possibility and willingness to contribute widely and generously to the common good" of humanity (23). Such a leadership role is not reflected in a nation's determination to keep out immigrants and refugees seeking asylum. This particular leadership rule is revealed, however, within a nation's willingness to help other nations address the economic, political, and social causes that lead so many of its citizens to leave their homeland in search of economic opportunities or safe living conditions elsewhere in the world.

Called to Family

That call to build a better world is first experienced within our families. How well we respond to that call is often determined by our personal experience of family life. Each person finds his true identity only in his social context, where "the family plays the basic and most important role" (*On the Development of Peoples*, 36).

Catholic social teaching emphasizes that the family is the most basic form of human community. It is within the family that we learn how to relate to others and begin the practice of living within a social setting. In the family, we learn that we are loved and are capable of loving others. It is there that we learn how to serve, to be responsible, and to be contributing members of a community.

Family life provides the opportunity to learn how to give and take and to work with others for a goal greater than ourselves. Learning how to get along with a sometimes disagreeable sister or brother is good preparation for working with persons in the larger community who may disagree with us on important matters. The family is a place where we can learn "to harmonize personal rights with other social needs" (*On the Development of Peoples*, 36).

Of course, not every family provides this idealized vision of nurturing positive growth in persons destined to become a contributing member of other communities and society. Some families are better suited than others to prepare young persons to respond to the call to community and contribute to the common good. Pope Paul VI observed that a family's influence may at times be "exercised to the detriment of fundamental rights of the individual" (*On the Development of Peoples*, 36). In some families, young people might sadly experience divorce, abuse, alcoholism, drug addiction, or disengaged parents. None of this takes away from the important role families can play in preparing men and women to be positive members of other communities and society. Still, it is important for all of us not to romanticize families and ignore their shortcomings.

For families to be a decisive influence in forming persons to be actively engaged citizens, they must be healthy. Catholic social teaching has long recognized that economic factors often determine how well families function. The first discussion of this was in 1891 in Pope Leo XIII's encyclical *On the Condition of Labor*. Pope Leo emphasized the need for workers to receive wages sufficient to support them and their families (see 35). In 1986, the United States Bishops stated that efficiency and competition in the marketplace should not be the only values guiding our economic system. More importantly, are "the way work schedules and compensation support or threaten the bonds between spouses and between parents and children" (*Economic Justice for All*, 93). It is no secret that families who are unable to afford needed groceries, medical services, or housing because of poverty or near poverty wages also often struggle with their own internal relationships.

Called to Participation

The call to family and community are related if we see the dynamics of family life as preparation for contributing to society and the many other communities to which we are sure to be connected. But what about the call to participation? And how is that connected to family and community?

One way to see this connection is to reflect on the dynamics that mark family life, particularly the way decisions are made within the household. For obvious reasons, parents usually take the lead in making decisions for the family especially when children are quite young. Notice what happens when children move into their teenage years. Parents will often hear the complaint, "Nobody listens to me. I never get to decide what I want to do." Whether this is true or

> Disorder in society is the result of disorder in the family.
>
> —St. Angela Merici

false in any family, these sentiments reveal the heart of the Church's teaching on participation. That is, participation is a right to be involved in decision-making processes that affect our lives. Of course, every right is accompanied by a responsibility—in this case, the duty to actually take part in making our families function well and making society work for everyone's benefit. The more a person is able to participate in this way, the better the chance of growing as a full, healthy human being. That teenager is on to something!

In Catholic social teaching, the right to participation developed rather late but its seeds were planted in the earliest social documents. Pope Leo XIII wrote that workers had the right to organize labor unions in a manner they judged best served their purposes (see *On the Condition of Labor,* 42). In *Christianity and Social Progress,* Pope John XXIII argued that if laborers were granted more decision-making power in the workplace, they would more readily participate in the governance of society as well (see 96–97). But, it was not until 1976 that participation was recognized as a human right. That came in an apostolic exhortation from Pope Paul VI, *A Call to Action*. As people become more educated, he wrote, they aspire to greater equality and greater participation—"two forms of man's dignity and freedom" (22).

If people are to take responsibility for their lives, they must have the freedom to make decisions about all aspects of their lives. Participation—being involved in decision-making—is necessary for the realization of human dignity. Full human development requires having a voice. It requires that every person have the opportunity to shape her life as well as the social context within which that life unfolds. *Economic Justice for All* states that "*basic justice demands the establishment of minimum levels of participation in the life of the human community for all persons*" (77; emphasis original). The ideal is for the largest number of people to have an active share in the governance of their society.

This teaching regards the best political systems as those that allow more and more citizens to be involved and to participate. In his encyclical *On the Hundredth Anniversary of "Rerum Novarum,"* Pope John Paul II suggested that if there is an acceptable alternative to capitalism and socialism, it will be one that offers citizens greater participation. Clearly, the Church values the democratic process because it leads to the participation of citizens in making political choices (see 46).

Connections to the Liturgy

The call to family, community, and participation is revealed in so many ways in the Church's liturgy. Liturgy is the worship of the Church. It is public worship. It is the family of God coming together to offer praise to God, to give thanks for the saving presence of Christ among his people, and to celebrate a shared, communal journey of the faith of a people redeemed.

Liturgy is the deepest expression of our call to community. This is particularly evident in the celebration of the Eucharist, a ritual filled with symbols and actions that keep before us the communal nature of our prayer. Many of the gathering hymns proclaim that we gather together to sing the Lord's praises. The opening procession of ministers symbolizes the people gathered for prayer. Many of our prayers and songs use the first person plural. One of the options for the Eucharistic Prayer emphasizes that God gives "life to *all things* and make[s] *them holy,* and [he] never cease[s] to *gather a people* to [him]self" (emphasis added). This is a gentle reminder that we come to Sunday Mass to worship and celebrate as God's people and not as isolated individuals. Even when we pray the Creed using the first person singular ("I believe"), we are making a public declaration of faith within the presence of a community who shares this belief. Worshipping together as part of the Eucharistic assembly is a response to the call to community worship. It is a call to deeper community.

The celebration of the seven sacraments reinforces the call to community. The sacraments are never private—even a wedding. Sacraments always take place within communal prayer and express the shared belief of the gathered community. At a baptism, the congregation renews its own commitment to life in the Church and then offers a visible and audible expression of welcoming the newly baptized into the same community. At a wedding, the community expresses its intent to nurture and support the engaged couple and then prepares to witness their sacramental union. Even the sacrament of reconciliation is often celebrated in a communal way. The faithful gather for a shared service of the Word and publically examine their consciences before participating in individual confession. After all have confessed their sins, the community regathers for a shared blessing and dismissal. In this way, the faithful are more likely to understand and realize that our failure to love not only offends God but leads to broken relationships within our communities. Sin has social implications. Sins of injustice, poverty, and prejudice harm community life. Even the sins we perceive to be the most private have a fallout that affects

> For you hear the words, "the Body of Christ" and respond "Amen." Be then a member of the Body of Christ that your "Amen" may be true.
>
> —St. Augustine

community. All of this is expressed publically and communally within the liturgy.

Liturgy also lifts up the family by helping spouses and their children learn the art of living in loving and supportive family units. Families sometimes bring up the gifts of bread and wine that will be used to become the Body and Blood of Christ. Members of the same family can be seen serving as extraordinary ministers of Holy Communion, readers, servers, ushers and greeters, or members of the music ministry. Outside of the Mass, other sacraments are celebrated in ways that provide a prominent role for the family. First communion, confirmation, and weddings are perhaps the best examples of liturgical celebrations in which the family surrounds and supports the individuals encountering Christ through sacramental ritual. This too is a part of the family life to which we are called.

The liturgy is the deepest reflection of our call to participation in community and family life. The first document of the Second Vatican Council was the *Constitution on the Sacred Liturgy*.[2] This document called for the many reforms that would be implemented in subsequent years, such as use of vernacular languages and simplified liturgical rites. The guiding principle for these reforms was participation. The Church realized that participating in the liturgy had a direct impact on the way in which a Christian lived in the world. And because of this, the liturgy must be accessible to the faithful. The *Constitution* said:

> The Church earnestly desires that all the faithful be led to that full, conscious, and active participation in liturgical celebrations called for by the very nature of the liturgy. . . . [I]n the reform and promotion of the liturgy, this full and active participation by all the people is the aim to be considered before all else. (14)

Liturgy must be accessible to the People of God. People should be welcomed to participate in the liturgy. They should never feel excluded. They should understand the liturgy and be able to pray

---

2. The Second Vatican Council was convened between 1963 and 1965. Called by Pope John XXIII, it was an international gathering of the world's bishops, respected theologians, and consultants reflecting upon the role of the Church in the modern world. The sixteen documents that came from this Council addressed contemporary peace and justice issues, the liturgy, the roles of ministers, and the nature of the Church.

in their own language. They should have access to the many hymns and prayers. They should know when to sit, stand, and kneel. They should be able to respond in whatever way is called for by the liturgy. They should have time to reflect in the silence of God's grace at particular times. They should have the option to reconcile with one another and to build their unity as the people of God.

The Second Vatican Council realized that it is only through the "full, conscious, and active participation" in the liturgy that "the faithful are [able] to derive the true Christian spirit." This was explored more fully in the *Dogmatic Constitution on the Church*, which stated that the liturgy, or more specifically, the Eucharist, "is the source and summit of the Christian life." It is the liturgy that forms the People of God (the Church) in their understanding of Christianity and, therefore, transforms the gathered faithful to go forth and participate in the world. Our Christian faith—expressed through Catholic social teaching and the liturgy— guides us in our responsibility for building up the common good.

Reflect ❖ Discuss ❖ Act

1. God makes us holy and saves us not merely as individuals but by making us into a single people. What does this mean in terms of your spiritual journey?

2. In our culture today, how might family life better prepare us for participating in society?

3. How might you live out a common good morality? What does that look like on a practical level?

4. Where do you see the right to participation lived out most fully? Where is this right not honored and respected?

5. In what ways do you participate in the liturgy fully, consciously, and actively? How does this lead you to participate in society fully, consciously, and actively?

The community of believers was of one heart and mind, and no one claimed that any of his possessions was his own, but they had everything in common. . . . There was no needy person among them.

—Acts of the Apostles 4:32, 34

Rights and Responsibilities

Almighty ever-living God,
in whose hand lies every human heart
    and the rights of peoples,
look with favor, we pray,
on those who govern with authority over us,
that throughout the whole world
the prosperity of peoples,
the assurance of peace,
and freedom of religion
may through your gift be made secure.

—Collect, Mass for Those in Public Office

I have a right to speak up. You have no right to take that right from me. Members of this community have a right to clearer information on this problem. How often do we hear ourselves and others lay claim to certain rights?

In our society and throughout Western civilization, individual rights are regarded with high importance. Human rights are best understood in relationship to responsibilities, duties, or obligations. Rights and responsibilities always go together. One cannot lay claim to a right without accepting his or her responsibility to respect that right in others. Rights and responsibilities also unfold in a social context. We claim rights and we fulfill our responsibilities in relationship to other persons and other groups, and always in community. Finding the balance between our duties and our rights is the key to the well-being of both the individual and the community.

Rights

Human rights are directly connected to human dignity. Human rights surround and protect the dignity of every person. Respect for human rights promotes the sacredness of human life. When human rights are threatened, the sacred dignity of that person is under attack. Human rights are essential to the development of the individual as well as society. Denying even a single right is harmful to both the individual and society (see *Economic Justice for All*, 80).

Human rights are universal. These rights apply to every human being living anywhere in the world. Any right that you and I might claim belongs equally to another person. These rights come from God and they can never be taken away—no matter what a person

> A person's rightful due is to be treated as an object of love, not as an object for use.
>
> —Pope St. John Paul II

does, he or she never forfeits the rights that come with being a person made in God's image. This is why the Church advocates against the death penalty. The Church is against the death penalty because a person who commits a horrible act against another person remains a child of God and is still able to reflect God's image, respond to God's grace, and repent of his or her act. Human rights, especially the right to life, are inviolable and cannot be taken by another person.

In Catholic social teaching, the first extensive discussion of human rights and responsibilities appears in Pope John XXIII's encyclical *Peace on Earth*, issued in 1963:[1]

> But first we must speak of [human] rights. Man has the right to live. He has the right to bodily integrity and to the means necessary for the proper development of life, particularly food, clothing, shelter, medical care, rest, and, finally, the necessary social services. In consequence, he has the right to be looked after in the event of ill health; disability stemming from his work;

---

1. In the previous chapter, we saw that the common good consists of everything individuals and groups need for their own fulfillment and for living a good life. What Pope John XXIII lists in *Peace on Earth* also defines the common good and reflects the basic rights one needs to fulfill themselves and live a fully human and dignified life.

widowhood; old age; enforced unemployment; or whenever through no fault of his own he is deprived of the means of livelihood. (11)

Documents issued after *Peace on Earth* include additional rights. One example is Pope Paul VI's discussion of the right to participation in *A Call to Action*:

While scientific and technological progress continues to overturn man's surroundings, his patterns of knowledge, work, consumption and relationships, two aspirations persistently make themselves felt in these new contexts, and they grow stronger to the extent that he becomes better informed and better educated: the aspiration to equality and the aspiration to participation, two forms of man's dignity and freedom. (22)

Another example is the right to immigration. In 2003, the Mexican and United States Catholic bishops issued a joint pastoral letter, *Strangers No Longer: Together on the Journey of Hope*. The bishops wrote that the goods of the earth are intended by God to meet the needs of all human beings. For that reason, if someone is not able to make a living in their own country, they have the right to migrate to another country in search of a better livelihood. Instead of building walls to keep such persons out, richer nations should find ways to accommodate this human right (see *Strangers No Longer*, 35). To put it even more bluntly, every person has the right to find in the world what she needs for a dignified life. "All other rights, whatever they may be, including the rights of property and free trade, are to be subordinated to this principle" (*On the Development of Peoples*, 22). In the United States, citizens regard private ownership as a supremely important value. Through the lens of Catholic social teaching, private ownership is less important than the rights of everyone to have their basic needs met. This suggests the need, at times, for society to make adjustments in how its economy is organized and in how its laws and policies regarding ownership best serve the needs of everyone.

> **If you are what you should be, you will set the whole world ablaze!**
>
> —St. Catherine of Sienna

Human rights are the minimum conditions for living together in society. In the United States, we most commonly think of rights as applying to civil and political matters—that is, the right to vote, the right to be free from discrimination, the right to freedom of assembly, and so on. Catholic social teaching, however, includes economic rights in this discussion: workers have a right to receive a living wage, everyone has a right to income sufficient for a dignified life, and therefore, people have a right to move from their homeland to another country (see *Economic Justice for All*, "Introduction," 17). Political and civil rights obviously are valuable and should be protected. However, it is equally important for us to make sure everyone in society has the income and economic necessities for a decent life.

In his contribution to this topic, Pope Francis emphasized the need to "broaden our perspective and to hear the plea of other peoples and other regions than those of our own country" (*The Joy of the Gospel*, 190). Unless we do this, we will not fully appreciate the rights that we ourselves claim, for these are rights that belong to all human beings. Even less will we understand the duties and responsibilities that come with recognizing that this planet belongs to *all* of God's children. Perhaps our failure to recognize this reality, explains the difficulty we have in recognizing economic rights, not only for Americans, but for people everywhere.

> Make justice your aim: redress the wronged, hear the orphan's plea, defend the widow.
>
> —Isaiah 1:17

Responsibilities

The first responsibility a Christian must attend to is that of caring for their own lives. This does not mean simply looking out for number one. Rather, the obligation here is that of paying attention to how we live in every aspect of our lives—spiritual, cultural, psychological, religious, social, and material. We are created to be fully developed, caring, and loving persons, and the responsibility to become that rests on each of us.

We saw in chapter 1 that Pope Paul VI saw every life as a vocation. "At birth a human being possesses certain aptitudes and abilities in germinal form, and these qualities are to be cultivated so that they may bear fruit" (*On the Development of Peoples*, 15). Developing these gifts and growing into morally responsible persons allows each of us to direct ourselves towards the destiny intended for us by our Creator. It allows us to become the wonderful persons God desires us to be—the persons we already are becoming. This is our first and most serious obligation.

Our second responsibility is toward our neighbors. Jesus' command to love our neighbor requires that we serve our brothers and sisters in caring and practical ways. As members of society, one of the most effective ways to love our neighbor is to promote the common good. Pope Benedict XVI pointed out that to truly love our neighbor means that we work for the betterment of society in ways that address our neighbors' needs (see *God Is Love*, 28).

> The kingdom that Christ preached and established is precisely that creation of his breath. It is made up of those pilgrims who traverse the earth with the responsibility of transforming history into the kingdom of God.
>
> —St. Oscar Romero

As individual members of society, one of our responsibilities is to defend all human rights, beginning with the right to life and including those rights needed to live that life in a dignified way until natural death. Most of us have various opportunities to do this through direct, charitable services—for example, volunteering at a local homeless shelter, participating in fundraisers, or fall yard cleaning for elderly or sick neighbors. We can also support the efforts of Church and other nonprofit organizations working to bring about changes in policies, laws, and programs that make it possible for persons to improve their lives on a more lasting basis. Most Catholic Charities provide such opportunities, as does the Catholic Campaign for Human Development and, in Minnesota, the interfaith Joint Religious Legislative Coalition. There are so many chances for us to contribute to the common good in ways that benefit our neighbors with the greatest needs.

Every Christian has a responsibility not only to acknowledge the rights of other people, but to do whatever one can to protect those marks of human dignity. *Peace on Earth* makes the point with simple clarity: "In human society one [person's] natural right gives rise to a corresponding duty in other [people]; the duty, that is, of recognizing and respecting that right" (30). That "duty" is to act whenever we witness or encounter an attack against human rights. The action we take may be to help bring forth change in large or small ways. For example, standing up for a student in school who is bullied, extending a hand of welcome to newcomers to our community who are criticized because of their ethnicity or religion, or writing a letter to the editor on behalf of others suffering discrimination, such as members of a racial minority group or persons with disabilities.

Those who are less fortunate also have the right to receive the necessary goods to live free of want—it is the Christian responsibility to ensure that this takes place. Pope John XXIII's document *Peace on Earth* states: "It is useless to admit that a [person] has a right to the necessities of life, unless we also do all in our power to supply him with means sufficient for his [or her] livelihood" (32). This could involve advocating for higher monthly payments in public assistance programs, especially when these payments have not been adjusted for many years. At times this might mean being willing to let go of certain benefits that come with our positions of privilege. Catholic social teaching clearly states that "the more fortunate should renounce some of their rights so as to place their goods more generously at the service of others" (*A Call to Action*, 23).

Our response to an attack against human rights can take many and varied forms. We may engage the issue as a concerned individual or join a larger community effort to address the threat. We may also challenge political leaders at any level of government to act on behalf of people whose rights are threatened or who are unable to secure for themselves what they need for everyday living.

The state along with its government leaders has a special responsibility to defend human rights. *On the Condition of Labor* presented this point. "Rights must be religiously respected wherever they exist, and it is the duty of the public authority to prevent and to punish injury, and to protect every one in the possession of his own" (37). The Church recognizes that Catholics may differ among themselves regarding the best way to respond to difficult social problems, especially when this involves political leaders. We must not differ, however, on our moral obligation to defend human rights and the dignity of every person.

It is not only the responsibility of the government to safeguard human rights. The Church also has a responsibility in this area. Her mission includes the proclamation that all have been redeemed by Christ and restored to loving and just relationships. The 1971 World Synod of Bishops saw in this mission a call to defend human rights. "This is the reason why the Church has the right, indeed the duty, to proclaim justice on the social, national and international level, and to denounce instances of injustice, when the fundamental rights of people and their very salvation demand it" (*Justice in the World*, 36). There is in the Church, as there always has been in the Judaeo-Christian tradition, a place for prophetic leadership.

All members of Christ's Body—those in the smallest parishes and those in the archdiocesan offices—must actively defend the dignity and human rights of all people, those within the Church and those without. Further, this Church's teachings and practices must reflect this commitment to justice in our world, and this includes the Church's public worship.

Connections to the Liturgy

This commitment to establishing just relationships and restoring human rights in today's world is present in various liturgical rites. The best example of this is found at the end of Mass. The presider dismisses us with a statement that often includes the words "Go in Peace." But we know that there cannot be peace without justice. This dismissal, therefore, implies that we go forth from the Eucharist committed to work for social justice—to work for the rights and dignity of all people, especially those who live on the margins of society. Without such a commitment, we cannot expect to find that peace in our lives nor in our communities. To be a member of Christ's Church carries the expectation that we lovingly care for one another. This has to mean more than simply praying for others and wishing them well. Just as important is the care we show for the material and social aspects of their lives, because the economic and social context of peoples' lives influences how well they do in their search for God.

This dismissal at the end of Mass is a sending forth. We are sent forth on a mission to bear witness to Christ and to the way our Christian discipleship calls us to live. This must include taking responsibility for the communities in which we live by celebrating the dignity and rights of everyone. This must include, as well, taking action to defend and restore the rights of anyone in our community or larger society.

Our Christian identity, rights, and responsibilities are given at baptism. Baptism makes us sharers in the priesthood of Jesus Christ. As such, we come to Sunday Mass not as spectators and not as dutiful subjects obeying a law about attending Mass on Sunday. Rather, as members of the universal priesthood we offer the Eucharist as one with the whole community, and we join in every aspect of this liturgy.

Baptism requires our prophetic voice. The prophet Micah wrote: "You have been told, O mortal, what is good, / and what the LORD requires of you: / Only to do justice and to love goodness, / and to walk humbly with your God" (6:8). This text beautifully summarizes the work of one baptized into the Body of Christ. As sharers in the prophetic role of Christ, we are to bring God's goodness, love, tenderness, and justice into our world. We do this in everyday life.

Our baptized Christian identity, finally, carries the responsibility of rulers. In this also we follow Christ in being present to minister to our brothers and sisters. The biblical model of ruler or king is that of one who tends to the needs of others. As sharers in Christ's kingship we are set on serving others out of love.

Baptism sets us apart from the world yet engages us in the world. Christian baptism likewise carries implications for justice and human rights. Baptism endows every Christian with a special dignity as adopted sons and daughters of God and with membership in a faith community. With this baptism comes the responsibility to recognize the same dignity and rights of all other members of the human family. By virtue of this baptism we have a "right and duty" to participate in the liturgy in which we "derive the true Christian spirit" (*Constitution on the Sacred Liturgy*, 14). It is our right to participate. It is our duty to participate. Likewise, it is our right to participate in the world because of our baptism. And it is our duty to do so.

> Christ has no body now but yours. No hands, no feet on earth but yours. Yours are the eyes through which he looks with compassion on the world. Yours are the feet with which he walks to do good. Yours are the hands through which he blesses the world.
>
> —St. Teresa of Avila

Baptism provides a new way of being in relationship with God, with others, and with the world. It changes who we are and how we are to live. Most importantly, baptism calls us to live out what we claim to be—a Christian. Our Christian identity and faith in Jesus must express itself in our worship of our God and in our willingness to build a world that is reflective of God's love, mercy, justice, and peace.

Reflect ❖ Discuss ❖ Act

1. Besides the right to life, what other right do you think is most violated in our society?

2. In what ways do you see yourself contributing to the common good?

3. When we offer the sign of peace at Mass, how might that gesture help us appreciate Catholic social teaching's call for us to work for justice in society?

The Spirit of the Lord is upon me,
because he has anointed me,
to bring glad tidings to the poor.

—Luke 4:18

The Option for the Poor and Vulnerable

He always showed compassion
for children and for the poor,
for the sick and for sinners,
and he became a neighbor
to the oppressed and the afflicted.

By word and deed he announced to the world
that you are our Father
and that you care for all your sons and daughters.

—Excerpt from Eucharistic Prayer IV for Various Needs and Occasions
"Jesus, Who Went About Doing Good"[1]

Didn't Jesus say, "The poor you will always have with you" (Matthew 26:11)? So why does our Church make such a big deal about poverty? It will always be with us.

To be clear, global poverty numbers are very high—probably around one billion. Some parts of the world have seen a decline in the number of persons living in poverty, like China and India. But elsewhere, particularly in sub-Saharan Africa, poverty is on the rise. Among today's poor are refugees and other migrants, a number that is now higher than at the end of World War II. With the reality of poverty, the Church challenges us to provide options for the poor and vulnerable.

---

1. There are ten Eucharistic Prayers from which the priest may offer at Mass. This particular prayer reflects upon Jesus' public ministry and his great love for the poor and the vulnerable.

Looking at Poverty

The extent of poverty and its effects on peoples' lives is well known, and not just by social scientists and other experts. "Today no one can be unaware of the fact that on some continents countless men and women are ravished by hunger and countless children are undernourished. Many children die at an early age. . . . Thus, whole populations are immersed in pitiable circumstances and lose heart" (*On the Development of Peoples*, 45). We know this. Everyone knows this. If we choose to continue to ignore the global phenomenon of poverty, more problems will occur. As Pope Paul VI warned, such inaction will call down on us "the judgment of God and the wrath of the poor, with consequences no one can foresee" (49).

> Love for others, and in the first place love for the poor, in whom the Church sees Christ himself, is made concrete in the *promotion of justice*
>
> —*Centesimus annus*, 58

Involuntary poverty is a threat to human dignity. Living without the basic necessities of life makes it more difficult to use our gifts and talents and become the loving, caring persons God created us to be. It can be difficult to take responsibility for our lives and contribute to the building up of our communities:

> But this sense of responsibility will not be achieved unless people are so circumstanced that they are aware of their dignity and are capable of responding to their calling in the service of God and of humanity. For freedom is often crippled by destitution, just as it can wither in an ivory-tower isolation brought on by overindulgence in the good things of life. It can, however, be strengthened by accepting the inevitable constraints of social life, by undertaking the manifold demands of human relationships, and by service to the community at large. (*Pastoral Constitution on the Church in the Modern World*, 31)

Church Practice and Teachings

Living the Christian faith includes a willingness to help people struggling with poverty. This has always been a necessary part of the Christian's life. The Gospel carries abundant accounts of Jesus' love for the poor and his expectation that his disciples through the ages will follow his example. The Parable of the Last Judgment and Jesus' command that we love our neighbor both call us to helpful, practical actions on behalf of persons who are marginalized and vulnerable (see Matthew 25:31–46). The Catholic Church has always responded to Jesus' teaching to love the poor. We see this in the lives of the saints, such as St. Francis, St. Vincent de Paul, and St. Teresa of Calcutta. Religious communities were formed to help the poor, such as the Franciscans, the Daughters of Charity, and the Little Sisters of the Poor. The Church has also instituted various organizations such as Catholic Charities, Catholic Relief Services, and the Catholic Campaign for Human Development.

Catholic moral principles supporting these practices are richly present in the Church's social teachings. These are teachings that have shown considerable development over their one-hundred-thirty-year history. The first social encyclical, in 1891, recognized the Christian's obligation to assist a neighbor in need by giving from one's excess or from one's superfluous goods. At this time, giving of one's excess was viewed as an act of charity and not of justice (see *On the Condition of Labor*, 19).

> Love the poor tenderly, regarding them as your masters and yourselves as their servants.
>
> —St. John of God

In the context of this book, acts of *charity* are "the acts we do to relieve people of their suffering." Think of Matthew 25 (Parable of the Last Judgment)—feed people who are hungry, give drink to those who thirst, care for the sick, welcome the stranger, clothe those who are without, visit those in prison. We also refer to these charitable acts as responding to peoples' needs with direct services. These are also known as the Corporal Works of Mercy.

Acts of *justice* take us to the next step where we ask *why* people are in need of food, clothing, shelter, and so on. Acts of justice require that we bring changes in society (economic systems, public policies, etc.) to make it easier for people to care for themselves and to have what they need for a dignified life. We also refer to these justice acts as responding to peoples' needs with systemic, social, or institutional change.[2]

The Second Vatican Council convened between 1962 and 1965. The Council was a gathering of the world's bishops to discuss the Church's role in the modern world and her response to contemporary situations. The findings of the Council provided a much stronger position regarding the Christian's responsibility to people living in poverty. The Council decreed that the more affluent must share from their substance and not wait until all of their own needs and wants have been satisfied. "This has been the opinion of the Fathers and Doctors of the church, who taught that people are bound to come to the aid of the poor and to do so not merely out of their superfluous goods" (*Pastoral Constitution on the Church in the Modern World,* 69). Then, to make sure no one underestimated the gravity of this statement, the Council fathers followed it with a quote from Gratian's *Decretum:*[3] "Feed the people dying of hunger, because if you do not feed them you are killing them" (*Pastoral Constitution on the Church in the Modern World,* 69).

> **You have been a refuge to the poor,**
> **a refuge to the needy in their distress.**
>
> —Isaiah 25:4

Undoubtedly, the most significant development in the Church's teaching on the Christian's obligation to the poor comes from Pope Paul VI. His encyclical *On the Development of Peoples* was issued in 1967, just two years after the close of the Second Vatican Council. In this document, the Holy Father speaks of the limits to private ownership in connection to meeting the needs of all people. Quoting the fourth-century bishop of Milan St. Ambrose, Pope Paul VI stated that the world is given to all, not just the rich. He warns that "the right to private property is not absolute and unconditional. No one may appropriate surplus goods solely for his own private use when others lack the bare necessities of life" (*On the Development of Peoples,*

---

2. A word of caution. Theologically, charity (or the virtue of charity) motivates us to perform both acts of charity and acts of justice. The distinction that I make is between the *acts* of charity and acts of justice, rather than between the *virtues* of charity and justice.

3. The *Decretum* is a twelfth-century collection of canon law compiled and written by an Italian Benedictine monk, Gratian.

23). The pope then challenges all Catholics to examine their consciences and ask themselves these questions (see 47):

❉ What would you be willing to do to improve the condition of persons trapped in poverty?

❉ Are you prepared to support efforts to help the poor by giving from your own pockets?

❉ Are you ready to pay higher taxes so that public authorities can direct more resources toward development in countries with great needs?

❉ Are you ready to pay a higher price for imported goods so that producers may receive just wages and payments for their products?[4]

Today, faced with controversies about tax cuts and trade embargoes, these questions are as relevant as they as they were fifty years ago.

It was Pope Paul's 1971 apostolic exhortation, *A Call to Action*, that has brought the greatest change in Catholic teaching about our responsibilities toward people living in poverty. The pope states:

> **What does love look like? It has the hands to help others. It has the feet to hasten to the poor and needy. It has the eyes to see misery and want. It has the ears to hear the signs and sorrows of men. That is what love looks like.**
>
> —St. Augustine

In teaching us charity, the Gospel instructs us in the *preferential respect* due to the poor and the special situation they have in society; the more fortunate should renounce some of their rights so as to place their goods more generously at the service of others. (23; emphasis added)

This is the first Church document that specifically uses the phrase "preferential respect." This preferential respect, or option for the poor, directs Catholics to assume an attitude or posture of "letting go" of the excess goods we could have by virtue of our

---

4. This question had been answered in his earlier document, *On the Development of Peoples*, when Pope Paul VI asked if we were willing to pay higher taxes, pay more for imported goods, or use our own money to provide assistance to people with greater needs than our own.

comfortable incomes and privileged positions. It means determining our own needs and wants by the absolute needs of people who have so little.

The United States Catholic Bishops revealed the practical meaning of the preferential option for the poor and vulnerable as it applies to both individuals and

> **Blessed are you who are poor, for the kingdom of God is yours.**
>
> —Luke 6:20

nations. The radical command to love one's neighbor as oneself leads to "the obligation to evaluate social and economic activity from the viewpoint of the poor and the powerless" (*Economic Justice for All*, 87). What does this mean for the choices we are expected to make? It means that whenever we are faced with two or more options regarding social or economic changes, we will support that option which provides the most help to the poor and the marginalized.

In the United States, health care policies are often debated. Usually these debates center around two or more plans (options) that backers claim would be best for our nation or at least for the majority of citizens. Catholic teaching regarding the preferential option for the poor tells us to get behind the proposed plan that we judge will bring the best health care services to those most lacking in financial resources.

The same can be applied to other issues—for example, passing just wage legislation or even voting in political elections. The option for the poor and vulnerable directs us to support legislation and vote for those candidates whom we believe will bring the greatest benefits to persons with the greatest needs. This does not mean we ignore the needs of people who are not poor. Nor should we neglect other issues facing society. The option for the poor does mean, however, that when we are deciding on an issue affecting all of society, our choice will be that which most favors those with the least resources—even if this option does not benefit us directly. The United States Bishops made two important statements on this point in *Economic Justice for All*: "As Christians, we are called to respond to the needs of *all* our brothers and sisters, but those with the greatest needs require the greatest response" (Introduction, 16).

Also in *Economic Justice for All*, the bishops, quoting Pope John Paul II, provide guidance for how we might come to the best choices:

The needs of the poor take priority over the desires of the rich; the rights of workers over the maximization of profits; the preservation of the environment over uncontrolled industrial expansion; production to meet social needs over production for military purposes. (94)

This kind of thinking runs counter to so many norms that shape our culture today—such as our national inclination to oppose raising taxes in spite of demonstrated needs; our tendency to ask political candidates "What are you going to do for me?" rather than "How will you promote the common good?" The option for the poor and vulnerable is countercultural. It is also a core teaching of our Catholic Christian faith.

> When someone steals another's clothes, we call them a thief. Should we not give the same name to the one who could clothe the naked and does not? The bread in your cupboard belongs to the hungry; the coat in your closet belongs to the one who needs it; the shoes rotting in your closet belong to the one who has no shoes; the money which you hoard belongs to the poor.
>
> —St. Basil the Great

Implications for Christian Living

The preferential option for the poor—the Christian's response to brothers and sisters struggling with a life of poverty—is rooted in our faith. There is, as Pope Francis stated, "an inseparable bond between our faith and the poor" (*The Joy of the Gospel*, 48). Pope Benedict XVI was equally clear on this connection between faith in God and the Christian's response to persons struggling with poverty. "Within the community of believers there can never be room for a poverty that denies anyone what is needed for a dignified life" (*God Is Love*, 20).

Catholic social teaching could not be clearer that the response to the poor should mark a Christian's life. Members of the Christian community will take different approaches in their response and actions. Most find the greatest comfort level in charitable acts, providing direct and immediate services to people in need. This should be the *minimum* response to poverty, both for individual Christians and for parishes.

Others, and hopefully their parishes and dioceses, will engage in acts of justice that seek changes in systems, structures, and policies that will benefit those in society with the greatest needs. This is *living out* the option for the poor. It also represents the kind of ministry that allows the Church—from the local parish to the Church universal—to proclaim the Gospel through its commitment to help the widows, orphans, and strangers, as we hear from the 1971 World Synod of Bishops:

> You who are rich, do you hear what the Lord God says? Yet you come into church not to give to the poor but to take instead.
>
> —St. Ambrose

> Action on behalf of justice and participation in the transformation of the world fully appear to us as a constitutive dimension of the preaching of the Gospel, or, in other words, of the Church's mission for the redemption of the human race and its liberation from every oppressive situation. (*Justice in the World*, 6)

Our response to the poor may take the form of individual actions. You might help to provide shelter at Church of the Week programs or serve meals at the Salvation Army or local food pantry. You might donate furniture to an immigrant family who recently moved to your community. Catholic Charities and many other nonprofit organizations provide a multitude of opportunities for Christians to practice their faith through practical service opportunities.

For others, the response might involve joining in social justice actions seeking a more lasting impact. More people, more resources, and more planning is often needed for efforts aimed at social change. Within the Catholic community there are opportunities for these efforts such as the Catholic Campaign for Human Development or the state Catholic conferences. Both organizations seek systemic change through their state legislatures.

Finally, whatever approach is taken, our personal lifestyles need to be evaluated. Do you live in a way that reflects Jesus' love for people who were marginalized by mainstream society? Does your life mirror Jesus' ministry and his great love for the poor? Are the poor welcome in your community? This approach is "the greatest and most effective presentation of the good news of the kingdom" (*The Joy of the Gospel*, 199).

Connections to the Liturgy

Participating in the liturgy of our Church requires that we respond to people's needs. This might sound a little strong, but consider the evidence. Many of the Scripture readings we hear at Sunday Mass recount how Jesus showed compassion to persons who had very little, who were sick, or who were excluded from society for various reasons.

> From the Eucharist comes strength to live the Christian life and zeal to share that life with others.
>
> —Pope St. John Paul II

The prophets of the Old Testament, whose accounts are often the first reading at Mass, insisted that being in right relationship with God meant helping the widows, orphans, and strangers. Some of these liturgical readings (see, for example, Isaiah 58[5] and Amos 5[6]) warn that worship (liturgy) is useless if it does not lead people to seek justice for the oppressed. Other readings proclaimed at Sunday Mass (for example, Isaiah 2[7] and Psalm 85[8]) remind us that the peace and harmony for which we collectively pray depends on the prior establishment of just relationships.

In the Lord's Prayer we implore for God to "give us this day our daily bread." How can we pray for our daily bread and not also ask God that daily sustenance be provided for all other members of

---

5. Selections from Isaiah 58 are proclaimed on the Fifth Sunday in Ordinary Time (Year A) and the Friday and Saturday after Ash Wednesday.
6. Selections from Amos 5 are proclaimed on Wednesday of the Thirteenth Week in Ordinary Time (Year II).
7. Isaiah 2 is heard on the First Sunday of Advent (Year A) and Monday of the First Week of Advent.
8. Psalm 85 is sung throughout the liturgical year. It is one of the seasonal psalms suggested for Advent.

God's family? How can we not pray as Jesus taught us and then go forth to help end the scandal of global hunger and malnutrition?

During the Eucharistic celebration, a monetary collection is always taken. The money is used for the support of the local parish, although some parishes designate a portion of this money for assistance to people in poverty. For example, the Benedictine monastic community of Saint John's Abbey Church in Collegeville, Minnesota, sends the collection taken from every other Sunday to a different program or organization serving the poor or working for social justice. The directions for the celebration of the Mass are also explicitly clear that during the Evening Mass of the Lord's Supper, "gifts for the poor may be presented with the bread and wine" while the traditional chant, "Where true charity is dwelling, God is present there," is sung (also known by its Latin title, *Ubi caritas*). These acts recall the collections St. Paul would take up in Greece and Asia Minor for the poorer church in Jerusalem (see Romans 15).

> Poverty is not made by God, it is created by you and me when we don't share what we have.
>
> —St. Teresa of Calcutta

When these acts of assisting the poor are integrated into the liturgy, they represent a powerful reminder of the connection between Eucharist and service to our brothers and sisters. Recall the ritual washing of feet during the evening Mass of the Lord's Supper on Holy Thursday. As we participate in this act of loving service we experience the Eucharist moving us to go out and use whatever gifts we have to bring relief to people with greater needs than our own, to live out the option for the poor and the vulnerable.

Reflect ❖ Discuss ❖ Act

1. What did Jesus mean when he said "the poor you will always have with you" (Matthew 26:11)?

2. In your own words, explain to a friend what the Church means by a preferential option for the poor and vulnerable.

3. During political election campaigns, how might you exercise this option for the poor and vulnerable?

4. Read Amos 5:21–24 or Isaiah 58:3–9. What does either of these texts say about your participation in the celebration of the Eucharist?

Whatever you do, in word or in deed, do everything in the name of the Lord Jesus, giving thanks to God the Father through him.

—Colossians 3:17

The Dignity of Work and the Rights of Workers

> O God, who through human labor
> never cease to perfect and govern the vast work of creation,
> listen to the supplications of your people
> and grant that all men and women
> may find work that befits their dignity,
> joins them more closely to one another
> and enables them to serve their neighbor.
>
> —Collect, Mass for the Sanctification of Human Labor

Ever find yourself wishing you could "strike it rich"? Win the lottery? Make it big at the casino? And, of course, never have to work another day in your life?

Many people share these wishes and would like to leave their jobs and the work cycle as soon as possible. Some people view work as a necessary evil—something they must do in order to put bread on the table. If they could find another way to meet their daily needs, going to work each day would be part of their history.

Catholic social teaching presents a very different view of working. The first Catholic social encyclical, *On the Condition of Labor* (1891), addressed the meaning of work and its place in the life of a Christian. That teaching has developed over the past 130 years and expounds more clearly upon the dignity of work and the rights of workers.

Work: Necessary and Personal

The Church does not regard work as an evil, not even a necessary evil. A good summary of that teaching is found in Pope John Paul

II's encyclical *On Human Work* (see paragraph 16). The Holy Father views work as an obligation because our Creator commanded it and because it is an important way for us to develop ourselves as a human community. Our concern for others also requires that we work—concern for our families, the community to which we belong, and the global human society. Appreciation for work is both necessary and personal.

Work is necessary in the most obvious way: we have to earn the money needed to live a decent life. Our wages or salary from our labor is the expected way for us to support ourselves, our families, or any other dependents who may be part of our lives. It is, as the bishops stated in *Economic Justice for All*, "the ordinary way for human beings to fulfill their material needs" (97).

We all get this: we need to earn a living. But, work is also a principal way for us to contribute to the well-being of others. Our labor provides us with the resources needed to help others, especially persons with needs greater than our own. It allows us to contribute to the communities and societies in which we live. "Work is not only for oneself. It is for one's family, for the nation, and indeed for the benefit of the entire human family" (*Economic Justice for All*, 97). And in that, notes Pope John Paul II, lies the moral obligation to work (see *On Human Work*, 16).

> **Our labor here is brief, but the reward is eternal.**
>
> —St. Clare of Assisi

Work is necessary. But Catholic social teaching also tells us that work is personal. Engaging in work—a profession, a job, a career—is one of the primary ways that each of us develops the gifts and talents God has placed within us. "Human activity is for the benefit of human beings, proceeding from them as it does. When they work, not only do they transform matter and society, they also perfect themselves. They learn, develop their faculties, emerging from and transcending themselves. Rightly understood, this kind of growth is more precious than any kind of wealth" (*Pastoral Constitution on the Church in the Modern World*, 35).

It is through our most common, everyday labor that we develop the gifts, talents, and intellect God granted us at birth. In working with others we learn to take responsibility for ourselves and those around us. Catholic social teaching has often proposed that workers be given a greater voice in workplace happenings as a way to develop their sense of responsibility. When this happens, workers are more likely to contribute to the well-being of their communities and societies as well.

The Value of Work

How do we measure the value of our work? Are some jobs or careers more valuable than others? Is the work of a brain surgeon more important—and therefore more valuable—than that of a sanitation technician? How about a farmer who produces our food or the person who works at the grocery store or fast food restaurant? Or a stay-at-home mom or dad?

In our society, we tend to answer these questions with a monetary value. While there are many factors that determine wages and salaries, jobs receiving the highest compensation are often regarded as the most valuable and important for society. The brain surgeon and the cardiologist seem far more esteemed than the farm worker. The simple fact is that we regard certain careers and jobs as more valuable to society; those "workers" are compensated accordingly. (This logic, however, does not explain why so many professional athletes receive salaries much higher than our surgeon friends.) In any case, the value of work is normally determined by the financial reward given to the one doing the job.

Catholic social teaching answers this question quite differently. In determining the value of work, Catholic social teaching respects the high skills required to do certain jobs as well as the education required, and the talents

> Come to me, all you who labor and are burdened, and I will give you rest.
>
> —Matthew 11:28

and commitments of those who pursue such careers. However, the value of work is not found in the *job* itself, but in the *person* doing the work. The value of one's job is not determined primarily by what one does, nor by what value society places on this work, nor by how much it pays. These are all important factors, and they do say something about the value of a particular job. But the most important measure for determining the value of any work is the dignity this work brings to the *person* carrying it out.

With this teaching in mind, we might ask different questions in determining the value of work. How well does this job match the gifts, skills, and interests of the worker? To what extent does this job allow the worker to use and develop the gifts given him or her by the Creator? Does the salary or wage paid provide sufficient income for the worker to live a decent life? Does the workplace environment reflect conditions appropriate for employees created in the image of God? The primary way to measure the value of work is by focusing on the dignity this work gives to the one doing it.

Work and the Just Society

Catholic social teaching regards employment that respects the dignity of workers as necessary for a just society. As already noted, these teachings began with an encyclical focused on the struggles of workers in the late nineteenth century. Since then, the Church continually has defended the rights of workers, especially their right to satisfactory and dignified employment.[1]

In his 1961 encyclical *Christianity and Social Progress*, Pope John XXIII presented this point with unmistakable clarity.

> If the whole structure and organization of an economic system is such as to compromise human dignity, to lessen a man's sense of responsibility or rob him of opportunity for exercising personal initiative, then such a system, we maintain, is altogether unjust—no matter how much wealth it produces, or how justly and equitably such wealth is distributed. (83)

Later Pope John Paul II wrote that human work is the essential key to the whole social question (see *On Human Work*, 3). The Holy Father continued this thought in his final social encyclical.

---

1. This message is often emphasized in the United States Catholic Bishops' annual Labor Day statement (which is posted on their website each year).

The obligation to earn one's bread by the sweat of one's brow also presumes the right to do so. A society in which this right is systematically denied, in which economic policies do not allow workers to reach satisfactory levels of employment, cannot be justified from an ethical point of view, nor can that society attain social peace. (*On the Hundreth Anniversary of "Rerum Novarum,"* 43)

John Paul II and all the popes who wrote on Catholic social teaching express a common theme—all of us are expected to work and therefore must be provided the opportunity for satisfactory employment. The lack of such opportunities presents an obstacle to the realization of human dignity. It must be clear that not only workers suffer—society as a whole suffers through lost taxes, increased unemployment compensation, and the expansion in public assistance. For all these reasons, Catholic social teaching considers unemployment to be an evil that must be avoided—a sin that "can become a real social disaster" (*On Human Work*, 18).

Satisfactory employment means that jobs are to provide wages and other benefits sufficient for the worker and his or her dependents to live a modest, reasonably comfortable life. This may seem vague and open to a range of interpretations. Yet the social teachings offer multiple signals on how we might measure "satisfactory employment." *Economic Justice for All* provides an example: "The dignity of workers also requires adequate health care, security for old age and durability, unemployment compensation, healthful working conditions, weekly rest, periodic holidays for recreation and leisure, and reasonable security against arbitrary dismissal" (103, referencing *On Human Work*, 19). The *just society* is one that provides satisfactory work, and an essential element of such work is a just wage. In Catholic social teaching, the just wage is a fundamental measure of whether workers receive fair treatment.

> The proof of love is in works. Where love exists, it works great things. But when it ceases to act, it ceases to exist.
>
> —St. Gregory the Great

Today in the United States there is much discussion and debate about the minimum wage. That conversation often seems to presume that minimum wage is a just wage. Yet the federal minimum wage—or that of any state in the union—does not allow workers to rise above the poverty level. Today hundreds of thousands of employees in the United States work full time, sometimes taking on more than one job, yet still remain in poverty. This raises the question: What constitutes a just wage?

Catholic social teaching never answers that question with a number—there are too many variables preventing specific recommendations for a numerical amount. The documents, however, do suggest a few basic measurements for determining a just wage:

❊ The wage or salary must permit a worker and his or her dependents to live a dignified life.

❊ The wage must also allow for savings, taking into account an individual's or a family's future needs.

The teachings also suggest how we might decide what that wage should be. The documents are clear that a just wage cannot be determined solely by the functioning of the marketplace, nor only by those with more power. Pope John XXIII stated "[a just wage] must be determined in accordance with justice and equity; which means that workers must be paid a wage which allows them to live a truly human life and to fulfill their family obligations in a worthy manner" (*Christianity and Social Progress*, 71). The ability of workers to live a dignified life is always at the top of the list in Catholic social teaching documents. Other factors include the contribution of each worker to the enterprise, the financial state of the company or employer, and the requirements of the common good locally, nationally, and globally.

Obviously, there is considerable room for interpretation on each of these factors; however, this does not change the most important criterion for determining a just wage—the need of the worker for a wage sufficient to allow him or her to enjoy a comfortable life. If such a wage could not be paid, Pope Pius XI wrote, "social justice demands that changes be introduced as soon as possible whereby such a wage will be assured to every adult [worker]" (*On Reconstructing the Social Order*, 71). A way for such changes to be enacted could be through the organizing efforts of the workers themselves. One of the workers' rights recognized in the earliest Catholic social encyclicals is that of forming unions—that is, the right to form associations to bargain collectively with employers. As Pope Leo XIII stated, it is the purpose of workers' associations (labor unions) to look out for the needs of workers and protect their rights. It is through the efforts of labor unions that the changes Pope Pius XI called for could come about (see *On the Condition of Labor*, 49).

With the right to organize comes the right to engage in labor strikes. In Catholic teaching the labor strike is viewed as the last but legitimate action for workers to engage in pursuit of changes they believe are needed, or in defense of their rights. Pope John Paul II summarized the tradition's position on labor strikes. "*One method* used by unions in pursuing the just rights of their members is *the strike* or work stoppage, as a kind of ultimatum to the competent bodies, especially the employers. This method is recognized by Catholic

> The LORD your God,
> may bless you in all
> that you undertake.
>
> —Deuteronomy 14:29

social teaching as legitimate in the proper conditions and within just limits" (*On Human Work*, 20). The proper conditions and limits the pope cites include assurance that the labor strike does not threaten essential community services. This is often a hotly debated issue when a strike is called for by unions representing workers in fields such as police and fire protection, nursing, or public sanitation. Workers in these areas certainly have the right to employ the strike, but they also need to consider the needs of society in addition to their own. The Church firmly opposes any interference with these efforts. "No one may deny the right to organize without attacking human dignity itself. Therefore, we firmly oppose organized efforts, such as those regrettably now seen in this country, to break existing unions and prevent workers from organizing" (*Economic Justice for All*, 104).

Church Employment

Given the Church's teaching on the dignity of work and the rights of workers, she has an important responsibility in safeguarding these issues within her own institution. The only papal social document directly addressing the Church's responsibilities to her employees—clergy, religious, and laity—is the 1971 World Synod of Bishops' statement, *Justice in the World*. This document, written by bishops from around the world, bluntly states what we should expect the Catholic hierarchy to endorse—both in word and in practice.

> Within the Church rights must be preserved. No one should be deprived of his ordinary rights because he is associated with the Church in one way or another. Those who serve the Church by their labor, including priests and religious, should receive a sufficient livelihood and enjoy that social security which is customary in their region. Lay people should be given fair wages and a system for promotion. We reiterate the recommendations that lay people should exercise more important functions with regard to Church property and should share in its administration. (41)

Connections to the Liturgy

The liturgy itself is work. This may seem surprising to you. The word *liturgy* comes from the Greek word *leitourgia*, which roughly translated means "the work of the people." In ancient Greece, this word referred to the offerings the wealthy made to the poor—it was a public work and referred to acts of service, an offering. Think about how this word, then, refers to our public prayer. Liturgy is the public expression of faith in which the baptized participate in the offering of Christ (his sacrifice) by offering themselves to him and to the world in service. Participating in liturgy, therefore, is cooperation in the work of God, both in our worship itself and the responsibilities that this worship requires of us in the world. The ability to unify our own offering with that of Christ's sacrifice dignifies our work in the liturgical rites and in the world.

The entire liturgy is the work of Christ, to which we are joined through our own prayer. As priest and liturgical scholar Paul Turner writes (speaking directly to the reader about Jesus Christ and the liturgy):

On the Cross he offered himself to the Father. At each Mass you are present again to this one sacrifice of Jesus Christ. Together with the priest you offer Christ to the Father, and together with Christ, you offer yourself. When you come to the Eucharist, you are bringing a sacrifice—the sacrifice of your very self. . . . You are offering to God all that you are.[2]

Our liturgical work, therefore, is self-offering. This is probably most evident at the Preparation of the Gifts. At this time, members of the assembly bring forth the gifts of bread and wine, which will be consecrated and transformed into the risen Body of Christ. These gifts symbolize the offering, the self-sacrifice, of the entire gathered community. And these gifts are the actual work of human hands, which is reflected in the prayer that the priest prays over these gifts:

Blessed are you, Lord God of all creation,
      for through your goodness
we have received the bread (the wine) we offer you:
      fruit of the earth
and work of human hands, it will become for us
      the bread of life.
Blessed be God forever.

The gifts of bread and wine which are about to become the Body and Blood of Christ come to the altar from God's holy creation; they are the fruit of the earth. These gifts also are the work of human hands. This prayer seems to presume worshipers' awareness of the human labor that brought the bread and wine to the altar—the growing and milling of wheat, the baking of bread, the careful managing of the vineyards, the harvesting of the grapes, and the making of wine. The dignity of this work is recognized

---

2. Paul Turner, *My Sacrifice and Yours: Participation in the Eucharist* (Chicago: Liturgy Training Publications, 2013), 7.

when it is credited, along with God's creation, for producing the sacramental elements for the Eucharist.

Our public worship also connects with the dignity of work and workers' rights in the world in other, more explicit ways. Petitions are often included in the Universal Prayer for laborers or for a particular category of workers, or for those who are unemployed and seeking work. The Eucharistic

> **Pray as though everything depended on God. Work as though everything depended on you.**
>
> —St. Augustine

Prayer prays that our eyes may be opened to those in need and that we may "comfort those who labor and are burdened" (Eucharistic Prayer IV: Jesus, Who Went About Doing Good). Many of the prayers for the saints recognize their good works and "apostolic labors"[3] for giving witness to the Gospel. Even St. Joseph has a special feast day each year, on May 1, which honors him as the model for all workers (St. Joseph the Worker). And in the United States and Canada a Mass may be celebrated each year on Labor Day for the sanctification of human labor.

Also during the liturgy, we pray the Our Father, which includes the line "give us this day our daily bread." No one expects our daily food to come from God without human cooperation or without human labor. The Lord's Prayer presumes that humans work to produce our food or to earn money to purchase it. This line also might be heard as a plea for people in poverty to receive daily food through the labor and generosity of their financially stronger sisters and brothers. There is a dignity in the work and the workers who make this possible which is acknowledged through the Church's liturgy.

---

3. Collect for the Optional Memorial of St. Turibius of Mogrovejo, Bishop (March 23).

Reflect ❖ Discuss ❖ Act

1. Do you commonly think of your work—job, career—as helping you develop the gifts God has given you? Do you often think of going to work as more than making a living?

2. As you think about the just wage, do you believe every working person should be able to make a decent living without having to work at two or three jobs? Why or why not?

3. What is your most common reaction to news that some workers are planning to go on strike?

4. The word *liturgy* means "the work of the people." In what ways is the liturgy "our work"? How is participating at Mass a sharing in the work of God?

5. Think about the natural, material elements that are used in the sacraments of baptism and the Eucharist. In what ways can our celebration of these sacraments shape our understanding of Catholic social teaching? How are these materials connected to human work? And to the work of our worship?

God has so constructed the body as to give greater
honor to a part that is without it, so that there
may be no division in the body, but that the parts
may have the same concern for one another. If
[one] part suffers, all parts suffer with it; if one part
is honored, all the parts share its joy.

—1 Corinthians 12:24b-26

Solidarity

O Lord, to whom no one is a stranger
and from whose help no one is ever distant,
look with compassion on refugees and exiles,
on segregated persons and on lost children;
restore them, we pray, to a homeland,
and give us a kind heart for the needy and for strangers.

—Collect, Mass for Refugees and Exiles

If you have ever been part of a well-organized group activity—school debate, dance line at a school dance, Fourth of July celebration, sporting event—you probably had an experience of solidarity. When solidarity is achieved, everyone is working together to achieve the group's goal or recognizes how much the success of the group depends upon each member doing well. Every participant is supported.

The word *solidarity* has long been connected to labor organizing efforts. "Solidarity Forever" is a popular trade union song dating to the early twentieth century, and "Solidarity" was the name of the labor movement led by Lech Walesa in Poland in the early 1980s. It is not surprising, then, that Pope John Paull II, who came from Poland, would be the one who most developed this theme in Catholic social teaching.

One Human Family

Solidarity points to the core Christian belief that we are one human family and responsible for one another. Each of us must contribute to the building up of this global community. In his encyclical *Charity in Truth*, Pope Benedict XVI wrote that, in our increasingly globalized world, our efforts to achieve national objectives must take on "the dimensions of the whole human family, that is to say, the community of peoples and nations" (7).

In Catholic social teaching, the notion of solidarity is closely tied to the fundamental principle of the common good—all those conditions (food, shelter, clothing, education, healthcare, and so on) of social living that people need for a dignified life. Solidarity draws us to see the common good in global

> As a body is one though it has many parts, and all the parts of the body, though many, are one body, so also Christ.
>
> —1 Corinthians 12:12

terms and not limit our vision to local or national identity. Solidarity helps us to see that what we desire for our own well-being we must be willing to support for people beyond our national borders.

Pope Francis sees an even stronger connection between working for our own prosperity and for that of other nations: "The principle of the common good immediately becomes, logically and inevitably, a summons to solidarity and a preferential option for the poorest of our brothers and sisters" (*On Care for Our Common Home*, 158). As is so often the case in Catholic social teaching, the Holy Father grounds this claim on the universal destination of the world's goods. That principle from the early Christian writers has implications for how wealthy nations relate to their less fortunate neighbors.

Pope Francis continues to unpack the meaning of *solidarity* in the *Joy of the Gospel*:

> The word "solidarity" is a little worn and at times poorly understood, but it refers to something more than a few sporadic acts of generosity. It presumes the creation of a new mindset which thinks in terms of community and the priority of the life of all over the appropriation of goods by a few. (188)

To be more specific and clear beyond any doubt, he adds: "Solidarity is a spontaneous reaction by those who recognize that the social function of a property and the universal destination of goods are realities which come before private property" (189).

It was, however, Pope John Paul II who most developed the teaching on solidarity in his 1987 encyclical, *On Social Concern*. He presented solidarity as a virtue through which we recognize—and live out—the moral implications of our connectedness to all members of this one human family. "When interdependence becomes recognized in this way, the correlative response as a moral and social attitude, as a 'virtue,' is solidarity" (38). Solidarity, he stressed, is not just a feeling of compassion or distress at the misfortunes of others. "On the contrary, it is a firm and persevering determination to commit oneself to the common good; that is to say, to the good of all and of each individual, because we are all really responsible for all" (38).

This "firm and persevering determination" is the stuff of virtues that he referenced earlier. In Catholic thinking, *virtues* are seen as "habitual actions conforming to high moral standards." These habitual actions, or good habits, require attention, determination, and practice. The virtue of solidarity is something we have to work at on a daily basis. Only with such an effort can we hope to develop this new mindset, which commits us to foster the common good on a global scale. Only with this effort can we hope to think and feel positively about nations and people beyond our borders and about abandoning narrow nationalistic slogans and rhetoric.

Solidarity calls us to act. In fact, the United States Catholic bishops define *solidarity* as an "action on behalf of the one human family." The bishops stress that "solidarity binds the rich to the poor. It makes the free zealous for the cause of the oppressed. It drives the comfortable and secure to take risks for the victims of tyranny and war" (*Called to Global Solidarity: International Challenges for US Parishes*, 4). Finally, in language that resonates with contemporary news reports, the bishops assert that Christians living the virtue of solidarity will open their hearts and homes to sisters and brothers fleeing terror, as well as migrants, whose labor makes possible our affluent lifestyle.

To be in solidarity with others is to act as if we recognize the human dignity we share with all of God's children. One of these actions is to seek changes in laws and policies that prevent people from escaping poverty and oppression. Another way to speak of solidarity is to recognize that the prosperity of one nation depends on the prosperity of all (see *Peace on Earth*, 131). No nation can develop itself or seek its own interests in isolation from the rest. An appreciation of that reality will lead to conditions favorable to the practice of solidarity.

In a world marked by extreme discrepancies between the rich and the poor, the practice of solidarity necessarily calls for sacrifice. This is a point frequently raised in multiple documents by Pope John Paul II. The Holy Father often reminded us that God's good creation is meant for all. This principle he extended to the manufacturing of raw materials into useable products. Any country that enjoys great resources must consider the needs of less endowed nations and be willing to share. Solidarity requires a global effort to advance the interests of peoples living in poverty—people unable to live in a manner reflecting the dignity of persons made in the image of God. Such an effort "involves the sacrificing the positions of income and of power enjoyed by the more developed economies" (*On the Hundredth Anniversary of "Rerum Novarum,"* 52). Clearly, the practice of solidarity takes us beyond acts of charitable giving.

> **The whole earth is a living icon of the face of God.**
>
> – St. John Damascene

Globalization

Globalization is difficult to define and its benefits are often debated. At the very least, it can be said that the globalization of the world's economy seeks to facilitate the trading of commodities and involves movement across the national borders of money, capital, and labor. The direction of this process is not always clear. Equally unclear is the question of who prospers from globalization and who is excluded from its benefits.

Pope John Paul II connected the conversation on solidarity with globalization. He warned about the new inequalities globalization might spawn and advocated for "globalization in solidarity, a globalization without marginalization." If this is to occur, then "we can no longer tolerate a world in which there live side by side the immensely rich and the miserably poor, the have-nots deprived even of essentials and people who thoughtlessly waste what others so desperately need" (1998 *World Day of Peace Message*, 4).

In spite of these reservations, the Holy Father saw promising opportunities with the rise of globalization. As the world's economies became more interrelated, people of different cultures, political systems, and ideologies might see themselves as one human family prospering from their growing interdependence. He saw the potential of the globalization of economies fostering the values of justice, equity, and solidarity (see 2000 *World Day of Peace Message*, 5).

Subsidiarity

Any discussion of solidarity should acknowledge the place of subsidiarity. This is a principle that has been part of Catholic social teaching since the late nineteenth century. Subsidiarity offers directions on how we should *practice* solidarity, especially in responding to people or countries with great needs.

Simply stated, *subsidiarity* means that "larger entities should not do for individuals and smaller entities what the latter are able to do for themselves." Government agencies of any type, for example, should not interfere in the working of families if these households are functioning well. A state government should not intervene in the matters of a city or county if these local governing bodies are functioning properly (see *On the Hundredth Anniversary of "Rerum Novarum,"* 48).

That said, the principle of subsidiarity also means the larger entity will offer assistance to the smaller or local ones when the latter have difficulty achieving their goals or undertaking necessary tasks. This assistance should not take the form of the larger, more distant entity doing the needed task, but rather helping the smaller one to accomplish their objectives and fulfill their responsibilities. Again, it is not for the larger, outside organization to do the job, but to help the smaller, local one function properly.

Subsidiarity presupposes that every individual and every private and public agency has something of value to offer society. This is best achieved by allowing private and public agencies to make these contributions under their own initiatives and guidance. The virtue of solidarity motivates us to assist generously other people and nations. The principle of subsidiarity offers important guidance for how this assistance is provided. That includes respecting the dignity of those needing assistance and promoting their own participation in the work to be done.

Solidarity as a Way to Peace

Catholic social teaching promotes solidarity among people and between nations as the way to achieve world peace. Solidarity seeks to improve the living conditions of all peoples, especially those who are poor and marginalized. In the absence of these improvements, we can only expect global instability and violence.

Those of us in affluent societies are fully aware of the hunger, poverty, and suffering endured by millions of people on this planet. Today's news, fed through a host of social media venues, makes it difficult for any of us to claim ignorance of these living conditions. Through the same news channels, the poor of this world also become aware of how their more affluent brothers and sisters are living. That growing awareness of their supposed inadequacies makes it more and more difficult to maintain peace (see *On the Development of Peoples*, 76). Pope John Paul II stressed that this increasing demand for justice among the suffering people of the world must be addressed by the community of nations:

> To ignore this demand could encourage the temptation among the victims of injustice to respond with violence, as happens at the origin of many wars. Peoples excluded from the fair distribution of the goods originally destined for all could ask themselves why not respond with violence to those who first treat us with violence. (*On Social Concern*, 10)

More recently Pope Francis stressed that "until exclusion and inequality in society and between people are reversed, it will be impossible to eliminate violence" (*The Joy of the Gospel*, 59). This is "a violence which recourse to arms cannot and never will be able to resolve" (60). It is a difficult task to end poverty and its accompanying violence. Pope Francis explains that in order for people to sustain a lifestyle that excludes others, a globalization of indifference has developed. These indifferences leave us incapable of the compassion needed to respond to the needs of the poor. Instead, we continue with our lifestyles as though the poverty and suffering in our world is the responsibility of someone else (see *The Joy of the Gospel*, 54).

In Catholic social teaching, peace is achieved only when all peoples recognize and accept that we are one human family and commit oneself to live in solidarity with all who inhabit this world. We are, of course, sinful human beings among whom there will always be tensions and conflicts. Still, it is important to see that controlling these conflicts and maintaining peace does not happen through a balance of power between enemies. Rather, peace is the result of our unending efforts to establish just relationships among God's people (see the *Pastoral Constitution on the Church in the Modern World*, 78). It is, as Pope John Paul II stated, "the fruit of solidarity" (*On Social Concern*, 39).

A commitment to peace is everyone's responsibility. When the values of human dignity and the common good are threatened, a prophetic voice must be raised (see *The Joy of the Gospel*, 218). That voice must be ours. It must be the voice of anyone who professes faith in Jesus Christ and claims membership in his Church. Ours must be the voice and the actions for building a world of peace through justice and solidarity.

Connections to the Liturgy

Perhaps no theme in Catholic social teaching is more clearly expressed in our Church's worship than that of solidarity. Each member of that body must look out for all other members or that body cannot be healthy. This is solidarity expressed through the prayers, symbols, and actions of our Eucharistic celebrations. We gather as one body. There is uniformity in what is prayed and how it is prayed through common song, prayers, responses, acclamations, gestures, and postures. Eucharistic Prayer III pleas to the Holy Spirit for us to "become one body, one spirit in Christ." The liturgy expresses unity among members of Christ's global Church which becomes the means—the sacrament—of unity and solidarity among all members of God's family.

Solidary invites us to look beyond our homes, our cities, our national borders and look to the needs of the entire global community. The ritual book that the priest uses for the celebration of the Mass, *The Roman Missal*, includes a variety of options for Masses that may be celebrated for various needs and occasions. These Masses are for specific situations and express our Christian mission to live in solidarity with all peoples. There are Masses for promoting harmony, for the unity of Christians, for persecuted Christians, for the progress of peoples, for the preservation of peace and justice, for charity, and for refugees and migrants. In total, forty-nine Masses can be celebrated for particular needs—all falling under the realm of solidarity.

> The Church continues being the good news, an event. The Church is always a community experience that leads people to listen to the wonders of the Lord and, in their evangelical roles as Christ's faithful followers, to denounce the sin of the world wherever it is found.
>
> —St. Oscar Romero

Specifically, the Universal Prayer expresses our mission to live in solidarity with one another. The title of the prayer itself points to the universality of the purpose of the petitions—to pray for global matters. Indeed, the Church requires that the petitions cover four categories of need: the Church, the world, the oppressed, and the local community. Petitions abound for an end to human trafficking, for those affected by natural disasters, for the poor and the unemployed, for the sick, and for the dying. Those who prepare these texts should always include current needs and issues. What we pray at Mass should reflect the current needs of the world. Our participation in the liturgy is therefore meant to change our hearts so that we live as Christian disciples. Hopefully, the petitions will inspire members of the assembly to act in ways that will solve, address, or respond to the needs that are offered to God. Prayer should always lead to action.

As the baptized, we belong to a universal Church, and we must be in solidarity with all members of Christ's Body, particularly its weakest members. Again, solidarity with all in the Church becomes both the symbol and means for us to be at one with all people. In so living, we offer a witness of breaking through the numbness, the powerlessness of despair, and the globalization of indifference. The liturgy empowers us to imagine that things can be different, and that we have a role in making that happen.

Reflect ❖ Discuss ❖ Act

1. How might we as a nation and as individuals best practice the virtue of solidarity?

2. How might our life in the Church guide us in living in solidarity with people beyond our communities, beyond our nation?

3. If peace is the fruit of justice and solidarity, how might we contribute to world peace? Where are the "handles" for becoming involved in this large and complex task?

4. Where in the Church's liturgy do you most clearly experience solidarity as it is presented in Catholic social teaching?

5. How does the liturgy send you forth to live in solidarity with others?

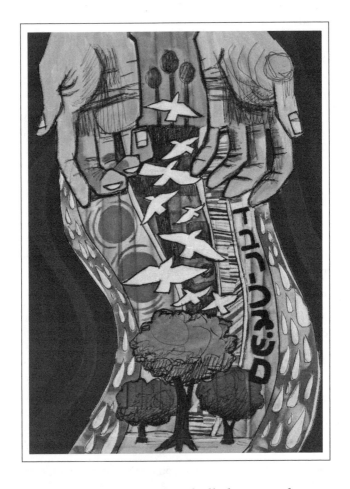

For in him were created all things in heaven
and on earth . . . ;
all things were created through him
and for him.

—Colossians 1:16

Care for God's Creation

For you laid the foundations of the world
and have arranged the changing of times and seasons;
you formed man in your own image
and set humanity over the whole world in all its wonder,
to rule in your name over all you have made
and for ever praise you in your mighty works,
through Christ our Lord.

—Excerpt from Preface V of the Sundays of Ordinary Time, "Creation"

The Lord rejoices in all his works! (see Psalm 104:31). What is your most profound experience of nature? A sight or action that seemed to awaken all your senses? One that moved you deeply and remains with you to this day?

That kind of experience in nature can lead all of us to give thanks and rejoice in the marvelous creation God has fashioned all around us. The psalmist seemed to think God himself celebrates all he has made. For our part, the best form of rejoicing and gratitude we can offer for this beautiful world is to care for it.

> Praise be to you, my Lord, through our Sister, Mother Earth, who sustains and governs us, and who produces various fruit with colored flowers and herbs.
>
> —St. Francis of Assisi

Creation Belongs to God

The starting point for any discussion about creation and humans' role in caring for it must be the recognition that creation belongs to God. The biblical witness could not be clearer on this point. "The earth is the LORD's and all it holds, / the world and those who dwell in it" (Psalm 24:1). The Book of Leviticus is even more pointed in reminding us that we really own nothing. "The land shall not be sold irrevocably; for the land is mine, and you are but resident aliens and under my authority" (25:23).

God's work of creation is an act of love. Not only does God create us; he also creates everything needed to support our life on earth. Pope Francis reflects on this as he explains his preference for the word *creation* over *nature*. Creation is "understood as a gift from the outstretched hand of the Father of all, and as a reality illuminated by the love which calls us together into universal communion" (*On Care for Our Common Home*, 76).

It is this understanding of creation that grounds basic Catholic social teaching about the universal purpose of the goods of creation. "God destined the earth and all it contains for all people and nations so that all created things would be shared fairly by all humankind under the guidance of justice tempered by charity" (*Pastoral Constitution on the Church in the Modern World*, 69). This summary statement from the Second Vatican Council is followed twenty years later by the United States bishops, noting the ethical implications of this principle:

> From the patristic period to the present, the Church has affirmed that misuse of the world's resources or appropriation of them by a minority of the world's population betrays the gift of creation since "whatever belongs to God belongs to all." (*Economic Justice for All*, 34; emphasis original)[1]

Clear in these statements is the claim that we can abuse or misuse creation—the natural world— in many ways. One is by harming it through environmental degradation. Another way we "betray the gift of creation" is by refusing to allow its resources to benefit the entire human family. We do this through our own lifestyles as we consume more than we need when other people lack necessities. We do this by supporting national policies that prevent people

1. Citing St. Cyprian, *On Works and Almsgiving*, 25, trans. R. J. Deferrari, in *St. Cyprian: Treatises*, 36 (New York: Fathers of the Church, 1958), 251. Original text in Migne, *Patrologia Latina*, vol. 4, 620. On the Patristic teaching, see C. Avila, *Ownership: Early Christian Teaching* (Maryknoll, NY: Orbis Books, 1983). Collection of original texts and translations. The Patristic Period refers to the writings of the early Church Fathers from around the first century to the eighth century.

in our own nation and elsewhere from receiving what they need for a dignified life. These practices go counter to God's intentions that the bountiful earth he created out of love would provide everything the human community needed.

The Goodness of Creation

A second point that must be part of any discussion on creation is to recognize that everything God has made is good. We read this in the first chapter of the first book of the Bible, Genesis 1:1—2:3. This creation story tells how our loving

> It helped me to look at fields, or water, or flowers. In these things, I found a remembrance of the Creator.
>
> —St. Teresa of Avila

God gave form to the world, separating light from darkness, dividing the waters, and effortlessly creating every living thing including humans. Seven times during these thirty-one verses, "God saw that it was good."

Elsewhere the Scriptures speak of the beauty and wonder of creation. "How varied are your works, LORD! / In wisdom you have made them all; / the earth is full of your creatures." (Psalm 104:24). Psalm 104 sings of all the creatures on earth as well as the sun and moon and storms—all of it dependent upon the Creator's continuing love.

Pope Francis writes that creation has everything to do with love. "God's love is the fundamental, moving force in all created things. . . . Even the fleeting life of the least of beings is the object of his love, and in its few seconds of existence, God enfolds it with his affection" (On Care for Our Common Home, 77). The Holy Father concludes that discussion by stating that humans can ascend from this good natural order so touched by God's love "to the greatness of God and to his loving mercy" (77).

Creation is also a privileged place for all of us to encounter God. The environment in which we dwell is sacramental. Through this ordinary, material universe we come into contact with our Creator. Ours is a "sacramental universe—a world that discloses the Creator's presence by visible and tangible signs" (Renewing the Earth, 6). As

Pope Francis wrote, God is present in nature. "The Spirit of life dwells in every living creature and calls us to enter into relationship with him" (*On Care for Our Common Home*, 88). This is a universe that calls for our respect.

We commonly recognize the practical need to respect and care for creation and the environment. Creation is limited and can be destroyed by thoughtless and selfish human actions. We are experiencing this now with the global climate change crisis. Economic considerations alone cannot guide our interactions with the natural world. We must also recognize the uniqueness of every living being and appreciate how every element of this world is interrelated (see *On Social Concern*, 34). On a strictly practical level, we can easily cause imbalances and disruptions in the environment that place needed resources at risk.

Our need for the goods of creation, however, can never be the only, or even primary, reason for taking care of this world with its many life forms. Catholic social teaching emphasizes that we should respect all living creatures because they are from God and they are good by their very nature. In his message for the World Day of Peace in 1990, Pope John Paul II made a stunning observation. He stated that the "respect for life and for the dignity of the human person extends also to the rest of creation, which is called to join man in praising God" (16). The Church's pro-life ethic must therefore extend to concern for life in the non-human world. Pope Francis pointed out that the tragic and continuing loss of species is more than a loss of potential resources for human benefit. Rather, this loss means "thousands of species will no longer give glory to God by their very existence" (*On Care for Our Common Home*, 33).

Other documents note that living beings in God's universe have value independent of their usefulness to humans. The United States bishops wrote that we should "treat other creatures and the natural world not just as means to human fulfillment but also as God's creatures, possessing an independent value, worthy of our respect and care" (*Renewing the Earth*, 7). Pope Francis further taught that "the ultimate purpose of other creatures is not to be found in us. Rather, all creatures are moving forward with us and through us toward a common point of arrival, which is God" (*On Care for Our Common Home*, 83).

Our Place within Creation

What is the place or role of humans within God's creation? Are we rulers over it? What does it mean to have dominion over creation? Are we part of creation? Do we have a role different from that of other living creatures?

The biblical stories of creation—Genesis 1 and 2—offer helpful guidance for answering these questions. The first of these stories, Genesis 1, speaks of men and women being made in the image of God, something not said of any other living being. The Creator tells the humans to be fertile and multiply and to have dominion over all living things (see 1:28).

The meaning of *dominion* has been debated over the centuries. Modern Scripture scholars, however, insist that to have *dominion* means "to rule in God's place and to rule as God would." That is, to exercise authority with love and compassion, to care for all that is weak and vulnerable, and to care for the earth. This is to include all of creation in our care for the poor and vulnerable.

> From a reflection on the primary source of all things, filled with even more abundant piety, he would call creatures, no matter how small, by the name of "brother" or "sister."
>
> —St. Bonaventure

The second creation story, Genesis 2, tells the story of God creating man and settling him in the Garden of Eden. There God tells humanity "to cultivate and care for" the earth (2:15). God then continued to create the other living creatures. All of these, including humans, were made from the same ground. In this story there is no mention of humans being made in the image of God. Rather, the connection between humans and all other beings is noted by having all of us created out of the dust of the earth. We are made of the same stuff and dependent on the same Creator. We are related.

Common to both creation stories is God's command for humans to care for the earth and all that God has placed within it. The

Scriptures are clear that we may use for our needs and our benefit what God has provided in creation. The biblical texts are equally clear, that in our use of the natural world we are to respect and protect it, and even to help make it flourish. Catholic social teaching reiterates this teaching. Human beings must see themselves as part of creation, not separate from it. As Genesis 2 metaphorically shows, we are made from the ground as are all other creatures. We are part of the created order, more *creatures* than *creators*. That said, we must also recognize and humbly accept the special role we have within God's beautiful creation. As both creation stories demonstrate, God has given us the responsibility to look after and to lovingly care for what he creates. "Human beings . . . are called to lead all creatures back to their Creator" (*On Care for Our Common Home*, 83).

> Some people, in order to discover God, read books. But there is a great book: the very appearance of created things. Look above you! Look below you! Read it. . . . God sent before your eyes the things that he has made.
>
> —St. Augustine

Cry of the Earth, Cry of the Poor

In Catholic social teaching, caring for the earth—the environment, creation—also involves caring for our neighbor, our fellow human beings. Christ's command to love one another can never become for the Christian a secondary priority behind our commitment to care for the environment (see John 15:12). In the Church's teachings, Jesus' command is expressed especially in terms of our obligation to respond to persons living in poverty. As Pope Francis said, "Today, however, we have to realize that a true ecological approach *always* becomes a social approach; it must integrate questions of justice in debates on the environment, so as to hear *both the cry of the earth and the cry of the poor*" (*On Care of Our Common Home*, 49). The deterioration of human living conditions accompanies damage to the environment. This deterioration affects most directly people who are poor and marginalized.

Today there is much concern about rising sea levels caused by climate change. Some coastal communities, like New York City and

Miami, are in a position to prepare for higher water levels on their shores as well as more frequent and severe storms. People living in poorer coastal communities, like Bangladesh or the Maldives, have fewer resources to deal with the approaching natural disaster. In some areas of the South Pacific, islanders (such as residents of Kiribati and the Carteret Islands) have already begun the search for new homelands.

Whether it is from climate change or any other form of environmental degradation, the people most affected are the poor and the vulnerable. They often live in areas most susceptible to such deterioration, whether caused by human actions or natural phenomena. Catholic social teaching always holds out to us the vision of a united creation— humans and everything else God has placed into the natural world.

> The earth is the LORD's and all it holds.
>
> —Psalm 24:1

We cannot care for one without attending to the other. "When we fail to acknowledge as part of reality the worth of a poor person, a human embryo, a person with disabilities—to offer just a few examples—it becomes difficult to hear the cry of nature itself; everything is connected" (*On Care for Our Common Home,* 117).

Caring for creation at this time of serious environmental threats requires more than quick technical fixes to separated problems. Addressing today's challenges calls for a long-term reevaluation of how we live and how our lifestyles are contributing to the problem or crisis at hand. An example of how we tend to name others as the cause of environmental problems is how we too often talk about global population growth. From the perspective of Catholic social teaching, however, population growth is not the primary cause of environmental degradation. "Consumption in developed nations remains the single greatest source of global environmental destruction" (*Renewing the Earth,* 9). Pope Francis expanded on this point:

To blame population growth instead of extreme and selective consumerism on the part of some, is one way of refusing to face the issues. It is an attempt to legitimize the present model of distribution where a minority believes that it has the right to consume in a way which can never be universalized. (*On Care for Our Common Home*, 50)

Connections to the Liturgy

The liturgy of the Church participates with the creative wonders of God. Anne Y. Koester writes:

The Church's liturgy forms in us hearts that care for creation by lifting up the sacramentality of the created world, following the rhythm of nature in marking time and celebrating feasts, making use of things of the earth, and leading us to bless animals, fields and flocks, soil and seeds, and to give thanks for what the earth has produced with the help of human hands. It also compels us to act with justice, protecting what has been entrusted to us and praising God through our actions.[2]

The liturgy is indeed sacramental. The ordinary things of water, oil, fire, beeswax, wheat, and grapes are used to become extraordinary vessels of God's grace in order to transform us and our relationships with God and the created world itself. All things are holy because God created them. And these holy things are used to worship the divine. Pope Francis offers an interesting perspective on how the liturgy, specifically the Eucharist, relates to creation. He writes that the whole cosmos gives thanks to God, and that the Eucharist is an act of cosmic love embracing and penetrating all of creation. The Eucharist, therefore, "is also a source of light and motivation for our concerns for the environment, directing us to be stewards of all creation" (*On Care for Our Common Home*, 236).

The great Easter Vigil—a celebration of the new creation granted in Christ—retells the story of salvation through the proclamation of several Scripture accounts. It begins with the story of creation and concludes with Christ's redemptive new creation. Salvation in

2. Anne Y. Koester, *Liturgy and Discipleship: Preparing Worship that Inspires and Transforms* (Chicago: Liturgy Training Publications, 2020), 98.

Christ is the recapitulation of all of creation, and participation in the liturgy is therefore a participation in this new creation.

The rituals and prayer texts themselves direct us "to be stewards of all creation" in the Eucharist (*On Care for Our Common Home*, 236). The Easter proclamation, which is chanted during the beginning Service of Light at the Vigil, recognizes the work of the bees that were used to create the Paschal candle, which stands as the primary symbol of Christ's creative redemption throughout the season of Easter:

> You gave us not only your Word through the Redemption and in the Eucharist, but you also gave yourself in the fullness of love for your creature.
>
> —St. Catherine of Siena

> On this, your night of grace, O holy Father,
> accept this candle, a solemn offering,
> the work of bees and of your servants' hands,
> an evening sacrifice of praise,
> this gift from your most holy Church.

In a similar tone, the Preface to Eucharistic Prayer II sings praise and glory to God who has made all that is and fills all creatures with blessings. If in our public worship we acknowledge God's tender care for his creatures, how necessary it is for us in leaving this liturgy to treat these same creatures with respect and compassion.

One of the Prefaces to the Eucharistic Prayer that is used during the season of Ordinary Time reminds us that all the natural world benefits from Christ's life, death, and resurrection. All things are renewed in Christ, who "by the blood of the Cross brought peace to all creation" (Common Preface I). This Preface reads as a response to Romans 8:21, which foretold that "creation itself would be set free from slavery to corruption and share in the glorious freedom of the children of God." Can there be a greater reason for us to rejoice in all God's works?

The long-standing tradition of blessings points to the responsibility to care for creation. The Church provides orders of service to bless people, fields and flocks, seeds at planting time, the occasion of the harvest, and animals. Blessings are even provided to bless the instruments used to till the soil and harvest the land.

The liturgy in so many ways expresses what Catholic social teaching tells us about caring for God's creation. Let us be careful lest by failing to value this beautiful world we inhabit we also fail to fully appreciate the Church's worship.

Reflect ❀ Discuss ❀ Act

1. What is your most profound experience of nature?

2. How comfortable are you with this biblical and Church teaching that we really do not own anything—that it all belongs to God? What are the practical consequences of this position?

3. What does it mean to be pro-life, according to Pope John Paul II and Pope Francis? Does this make sense to you?

4. As already noted in this resource, there are many parts of the Mass in which we are reminded of God's love for all of creation. Think about these moments. Name them. How do they help you appreciate more deeply the Catholic social teaching about our obligation to care for the environment?

5. The sacrament of baptism uses water as a symbol for the cleansing of sin. What happens in the imagination of worshippers when their experience of water is that of a threat? How do they view the rituals and symbols of this sacrament when they regularly read news accounts of water being contaminated by farm chemicals and suburban lawn runoff? How does this change or enhance your view of liturgy and creation?

CATHOLIC SOCIAL TEACHING DOCUMENTS

Vatican Social Documents

Below is a list of the major documents on Catholic social teaching issued by the Vatican. Many of these documents can be found online, especially on the Vatican website.

Latin Title	English Title	Pope, Council, Synod	Date of Issue
Rerum novarum	*On the Condition of Labor*	Pope Leo XIII	1891
Quadragesimo anno	*On the Reconstruction of the Social Order*	Pope Pius XI	1931
Mater et magistra	*Christianity and Social Progress*	Pope John XXIII	1961
Pacem in terris	*Peace on Earth*	Pope John XXIII	1963
Gaudium et spes	*Pastoral Constitution on the Church in the Modern World*	Second Vatican Council	1965
Populorum progressio	*On the Development of Peoples*	Pope Paul VI	1967
Octogesima adveniens	*A Call to Action*	Pope Paul VI	1971
Justitia in mundo	*Justice in the World*	Synod of Bishops	1971
Evangelii nuntiandi	*Evangelization in the Modern World*	Pope Paul VI	1975
Laborem exercens	*On Human Work*	Pope John Paul II	1981
Sollicitudo rei socialis	*On Social Concern*	Pope John Paul II	1987
Centesimus annus	*On the Hundredth Anniversary of "Rerum Novarum"*	Pope John Paul II	1991
Caritas in veritate	*In Charity and Truth*	Pope Benedict XVI	2009
Evangelii gaudium	*The Joy of the Gospel*	Pope Francis	2013
Laudato si'	*On Care for Our Common Home*	Pope Francis	2015

Other Vatican Documents

The following documents, though not specifically *social* documents, are also helpful in understanding the nature of Church, liturgy, and social teaching.

Latin Title	English Title	Pope, Council, Synod	Date of Issue
Lumen gentium	*Dogmatic Constitution on the Church*	Second Vatican Council	1964
Dignitatis humanae	*Declaration on Religious Freedom*	Second Vatican Council	1965
	The Church and Racism: Toward a More Fraternal Society	Pontifical Council for Justice and Peace	1988
Veritatis splendor	*On Some Fundamental Questions of the Church's Moral Teaching*	Pope John Paul II	1993
Evangelium vitae	*The Gospel of Life*	Pope John Paul II	1995
Fides et ratio	*Faith and Reason*	Pope John Paul II	1998
Ecclesia in America	*The Church in America*	Pope John Paul II	1999
	Doctrinal Note on Some Questions regarding the Participation of Catholics in Political Life	Congregation for the Doctrine of the Faith	2002
	Compendium of the Social Doctrine of the Church	Pontifical Council for Justice and Peace	2004
Deus caritas est	*God Is Love*	Pope Benedict XVI	2005
Sacramentum caritatis	*The Sacrament of Charity*	Pope Benedict XVI	2007
Dignitas personae	*The Dignity of a Person*	Congregation for the Doctrine of the Faith	2008
Lumen fidei	*On the Light of Faith*	Pope Francis	2013
Amoris laetitia	*On Love in the Family*	Pope Francis	2016
Gaudete et exsultate	*On the Call to Holiness in Today's World*	Pope Francis	2018

United States Bishops

The United States bishops have issued numerous documents related to Catholic social teaching on issues such as racism, immigration, abortion, creation, and voting. Below is a list of pastoral letters from the US bishops, which can be found online: http://www.usccb.org/beliefs-and-teachings/what-we-believe/catholic-social-teaching/foundational-documents.cfm. You may also visit this website to learn more about the many issues surrounding our nation and our world, the Catholic response, and what you can do to pray and act: http://www.usccb.org/issues-and-action/index.cfm.

Title	Date of Issue
Pastoral Statement on Persons with Disabilities	1978
Brothers and Sisters to Us	1979
In the Name of Peace: Collective Statements on War and Peace	1919–1980
The Challenge of Peace	1983
Economic Justice for All	1986
Homelessness and Housing	1988
Called to Compassion and Responsibility	1989
A Century of Social Teaching	1990
New Slavery, New Freedom	1990
Renewing the Earth	1991
When I Call for Help: A Pastoral Response to Violence against Women	1992
The Harvest of Justice Is Sown in Peace	1993
Communities of Salt and Light	1993
The Cries of the Poor Are Still with Us	1995
A Decade after "Economic Justice for All"	1995
Sowing Weapons of War	1995
A Catholic Framework for Economic Life	1996
Called to Global Solidarity	1997
Everyday Christianity: To Hunger and Thirst for Justice	1998
Living the Gospel of Life	1998

Title (continued from previous page)	Date of Issue
In All Things Charity: A Pastoral Challenge for the New Millennium	1999
Everyday Christianity: To Hunger and Thirst for Justice	1999
Welcoming the Stranger among Us: Unity in Diversity	2000
Global Climate Change: A Plea for Dialogue, Prudence, and the Common Good	2001
A Place at the Table: A Catholic Recommitment to Overcome Poverty and to Respect the Dignity of All God's Children	2001
A Matter of the Heart	2002
Strangers No Longer: Together on the Journey of Hope	2003
For I Was Hungry and You Gave Me Food: Catholic Reflections on Food, Farmers, and Farmworkers	2003
A Culture of Life and the Penalty of Death	2005
Respecting the Just Rights of Workers	2009
Forming Consciences for Faithful Citizenship	2015; 2011; 2007
Open Wide Our Hearts: The Enduring Call to Love	2018